THE ESSENTIAL PREPPERS NATURAL MEDICINE GUIDE

3 in 1 Navigate the Path to Natural Wellness with Comprehensive Guides on Crafting Your Own Medicinal Remedies, Promoting Sustainability and Self-Reliance

Terri Neal

Table of Contents

BOOK 1: FOUNDATIONS OF PREPPER'S NATURAL MEDICINE

SURVIVAL BOTANICA: ESSENTIALS OF PREPPER'S NATURAL MEDICINE

CHAPTER 1: THE PREPPER'S PHARMACY

Welcome to your new role as the caretaker of your own health and well-being. In the realm of preparedness, the mastery of natural medicine starts with a deep understanding of the tools and resources that Mother Nature generously provides. Here, in your herbal garden or the untouched wilds around you, lies your very own pharmacy—one that empowers you to maintain health sovereignty even when modern conveniences are beyond reach.

Imagine stepping into a lush sanctuary where each plant offers more than just aesthetic pleasure; they present solutions to common ailments that afflict many households. Through learning to identify, harvest, and utilize these plants, you're not just preparing for uncertain times—you're also taking proactive steps toward a healthier lifestyle today.

This chapter, "The Prepper's Pharmacy," is designed to bridge the gap between the natural world and your home medicine cabinet. It begins with understanding the fundamental characteristics of medicinal plants, exploring how and why they work. Then, we'll guide you through setting up your own herbal garden, ensuring that you grow the most beneficial plants with respect to your local climate and soil conditions. Finally, we delve into the ethical considerations and safety measures necessary for foraging in the wild, ensuring that you sustain both your health and the environment. As we journey through this chapter together, remember that this is more than just a collection of names and properties. It's an invitation to forge a connection with the earth, to turn to the wisdom of the past, and to reclaim a legacy of wellness that many have forgotten. Welcome to your first step toward becoming a seasoned herbal prepper.

1. Understanding Medicinal Plants

In the heart of every natural pharmacy, medicinal plants stand as the foundation, rooted in centuries of traditional knowledge and backed by modern science. These plants are not just flora; they are the ancient allies of humankind, offering their healing virtues to those who know how to harness their power. Understanding these plants goes beyond mere identification. It involves a deep dive into their history, biology, and the symbiotic relationship they can share with us—if we choose to learn their secrets.

From the lush, overgrown forests to the humble backyard garden, medicinal plants are ubiquitous, thriving in diverse ecosystems and adapted to various climates and soils. Each species carries a unique profile of active compounds that interact with the human body in specific ways. For instance, the willow tree, a common sight along rivers and in damp forests, offers us salicin, which the body converts into salicylic acid, a precursor of aspirin. This natural pain reliever has been used for centuries to alleviate fever and inflammation, a testament to nature's pharmacy at our fingertips.

However, cultivating a deep understanding of medicinal plants requires more than recognizing their therapeutic properties. One must also consider the ecological roles these plants play. They are not merely static entities in their habitats but dynamic participants in ecological networks. Their interactions with the soil, pollinators, and other plants can teach us much about how to grow and use them sustainably. For example, understanding that lavender attracts pollinators such as bees can help us plan gardens that support local wildlife while providing us with resources for natural remedies.

Learning to identify medicinal plants is the first practical step in utilizing their benefits. This involves more than memorizing appearances; it's about observing them through the seasons and understanding how they change under various environmental conditions. Field guides and botanical gardens can be invaluable resources, but nothing replaces the hands-on experience of walking through a landscape and observing plants in their natural settings. This immersive approach helps solidify recognition and deepens our connection to the plant world.

The biology of medicinal plants is equally fascinating. Many people are surprised to learn about the complexity of plant chemistry and how plants produce the compounds that can be therapeutic. For instance, the concept of secondary metabolites, which are chemicals produced by plants not for their growth but primarily for defending against predators, attracting pollinators, or mitigating disease. These secondary metabolites are often the source of medicinal properties. Phytochemicals like flavonoids, terpenes, and alkaloids have various effects on the human body, from reducing inflammation to combating pathogens.

Moreover, understanding these compounds is not merely academic. It guides practical applications such as the best times for harvesting. Plants synthesize certain chemicals at specific phases in their life cycle or even at particular times of the day. For instance, harvesting herbs early in the morning after the dew has evaporated but before the sun depletes their essential oils can optimize the potency of a remedy.

The therapeutic uses of medicinal plants are vast and varied. Many plants have multifunctional applications, addressing not just physical ailments but also promoting mental and emotional well-being. Lavender, for example, is renowned not only for its antiseptic and anti-inflammatory properties but also for its ability to alleviate stress and promote better sleep. Similarly, St. John's wort, while commonly used for its antidepressant qualities, also has potent antiviral and antibacterial properties, making it a staple in any natural medicine cabinet.

Responsible sourcing of medicinal plants is a critical aspect of herbal medicine. As the interest in natural remedies grows, so does the pressure on plant populations. Ethical foraging and cultivation become paramount to ensure sustainability. Ethical foraging involves understanding which parts of the plant to harvest and how much can be taken without harming the plant or its ecosystem. For instance, one should never uproot a whole plant unless it's abundant and part of a managed harvest. Cultivating your own medicinal plants not only alleviates pressure on wild populations but also provides the freshest, most potent materials for remedies.

Finally, while the allure of natural remedies is strong, it is essential to approach herbal medicine with a balanced perspective. Not all plants are safe for all people, and interactions with pharmaceuticals must be considered. Educating oneself about potential side effects and contraindications is crucial. This is where bridging traditional knowledge with scientific research becomes invaluable. Consulting with healthcare professionals knowledgeable in both conventional and herbal medicine can provide a safe and effective way to integrate these ancient remedies into modern health practices.

In this journey through the world of medicinal plants, we rekindle a relationship with nature that is often lost in the hustle of modern life. We learn not only to care for our bodies in the most natural ways possible but also to sustain the health of the planet that nurtures these botanicals. Understanding medicinal plants is thus a dual path of healing—both personal and planetary.

2. Setting Up Your Herbal Garden

Starting your own herbal garden is more than a venture into gardening; it's a step towards resilience and independence in managing your health. As you plan to set up your herbal sanctuary, consider it not just a collection of plants but a living pharmacy that will grow alongside you, adaptable and robust.

The first step is selecting a suitable site for your garden. You'll want a location that receives adequate sunlight—at least six hours a day—as many herbs thrive in full sun. However, if your region is particularly hot, some afternoon shade might be necessary to prevent scorching. Accessibility is also crucial; ensure your garden is easy to reach for regular maintenance and harvesting. Consider proximity to water sources as well, since carrying water across long distances can become a tiresome chore.

Soil quality cannot be overstated. Most medicinal herbs prefer well-drained soil rich in organic matter. You might need to work the soil by adding compost or aged manure, which will not only improve soil structure but also enhance its nutrient content. A simple soil test can reveal pH and nutrient levels, helping you adjust the soil conditions to suit your specific plants. Generally, a slightly acidic to neutral pH works well for a diverse range of herbs.

Plant selection is the heart of your herbal garden. Choose plants based on their medicinal value as well as their adaptability to your climate and soil. Start with the basics like lavender for its calming properties, chamomile for soothing teas, and peppermint for digestive health. As your skills and confidence grow, you can expand your garden to include more specialized plants like echinacea for immune support and valerian for sleep enhancement. Always consider your household's specific health needs when choosing which herbs to cultivate.

Planting can be done from seeds or seedlings, depending on your preference and the plant's requirements. Some herbs, like parsley and basil, are easily grown from seeds directly sowed into the garden. Others, such as rosemary and thyme, are better started as seedlings or cuttings to ensure they thrive. When planting, give each herb enough space to grow without competition for sunlight, air, or nutrients. This not only encourages healthy growth but also reduces the risk of disease. Watering your garden demands attention to detail. Most herbs prefer soil that is moist but not waterlogged. Over-watering can be just as detrimental as under-watering, leading to root rot or fungal infections. Establish a consistent watering schedule that keeps the soil appropriately moist, and adjust based on rainfall and temperature changes.

Mulching is beneficial in retaining soil moisture and suppressing weeds. Organic mulches like straw or bark chips can also add to the soil's nutrient profile as they decompose. However, ensure the mulch does not touch the plant stems directly to avoid moisture-related diseases.

Regular maintenance involves more than watering and weeding. Observing your plants closely helps in early detection of any issues like pest infestations or diseases, which can often be managed naturally without resorting to harsh chemicals. Companion planting can be a natural deterrent to pests; for example, planting garlic near roses can help repel aphids.

Harvesting herbs is as much about timing as it is about technique. Most herbs yield the highest concentration of essential oils just before they bloom, making this the optimal time for harvesting. Use sharp, clean shears to cut only what you need, encouraging the plants to continue producing throughout the season. Drying or immediately using fresh herbs for preparations can maximize their medicinal properties.

Winter preparation is vital for perennial herbs. In colder climates, some herbs will need protection from freezing temperatures. Mulching around the base of the plants can help insulate roots from frost, and some may need to be brought indoors or into a greenhouse.

Finally, remember that your herbal garden is a living entity that requires attention, care, and respect. It's not just about the utility of the herbs but also about building a relationship with nature that can be profoundly satisfying and healing. As you tend to your garden, you'll find that it not only provides medicinal benefits but also becomes a sanctuary of tranquility—an oasis where you can reconnect with the earth and restore your spirits.

Through these steps, your garden will flourish, providing not only a source of natural remedies but also a profound sense of achievement and autonomy in your journey toward sustainable living and health.

3. Wild Foraging Safety and Ethics

Embracing the role of a forager connects us with our ancestral roots, allowing us to walk the paths once trodden by those who lived off the land long before the advent of supermarkets and pharmacies. Wild foraging for medicinal plants not only enriches our connection to the environment but also imbues us with a profound responsibility towards both our health and the health of our ecosystems. Understanding the safety and ethical considerations of foraging is crucial for anyone who wishes to integrate these ancient practices into modern life. Safety in foraging is paramount, as the natural world is as fraught with hazards as it is abundant with remedies. The first rule of foraging is to never harvest or consume a plant unless you are absolutely certain of its identity. Mistaking one plant for another can be a harmless error—or a fatal one. Invest time in learning from experienced foragers, attending workshops, and studying field guides. Digital apps can aid identification, but they should complement rather than replace the deeper learning obtained from books and human mentors.

Alongside correct identification, consider the plant's environment. Plants growing near roads, industrial areas, or sprayed fields may be contaminated with pollutants or pesticides, making them unsuitable for medicinal use. Always forage in clean, uncontaminated environments, and understand the history of the land to ensure the purity of your harvest.

Foraging must also respect the plant's life cycle and its role in the ecosystem. Learn to recognize the stages of growth and only harvest when a plant is mature enough to withstand some of its parts being taken. For example, gathering leaves or flowers is generally less impactful than uprooting or taking large portions of the plant.

The ethics of foraging extend beyond safety and into sustainability. It is our duty to ensure that our actions today do not deplete resources for future generations. A responsible forager always adheres to the principle of moderation—taking only what is needed and leaving enough behind to allow the plant population to regenerate. A good rule of thumb is to harvest no more than one-third of a patch or area. This ensures that enough plants remain to reproduce and continue supporting the local wildlife that depend on them.

In addition to conservation of plant populations, ethical foraging also involves respecting other foragers and the local community. This includes recognizing and adhering to local laws and regulations regarding foraging. Many areas have specific guidelines about what can be foraged and where. Some places may be protected, requiring permits, or completely off-limits to foraging to protect endangered species or fragile ecosystems. Always be informed about the regulations in your foraging area to avoid legal infractions and potential damage to the environment.

Building a reciprocal relationship with nature is also a key aspect of ethical foraging. This means not only taking from the land but also giving back. Practices such as scattering seeds to promote growth and participating in local conservation efforts can enhance the health of the ecosystems from which we harvest. By contributing to the health of the land, we ensure that it continues to be a bountiful source for future generations.

Practicing safe disposal of waste is another important aspect of foraging ethics. When in the wild, adopt the leave-no-trace principles—pack out everything you bring in, and be mindful of your impact on the natural surroundings. Disturbing the soil minimally, avoiding trampling undergrowth, and leaving areas as undisturbed as possible are all practices that preserve the integrity of the wild spaces we enjoy.

Additionally, sharing knowledge and fostering community around foraging can enhance its ethical practice. By teaching others about safe and sustainable foraging, we spread awareness and cultivate a community of responsible foragers. Workshops, guided walks, and foraging groups can be invaluable for beginners and experts alike, providing spaces for knowledge exchange and mutual support.

In embracing wild foraging, you engage in an activity that feeds not just the body, but also the soul. It is a pursuit that demands mindfulness and respect—qualities that ensure safety and sustainability. As you step into the wild with a basket in hand, you are continuing a human practice as old as time, bridging the gap between our past and our future. Through this practice, we not only sustain our bodies with natural medicines but also deepen our relationship with the earth, crafting a legacy of stewardship and respect for the natural world.

4. Harnessing Seasonal Cycles for Medicinal Harvesting

Harnessing the seasonal cycles for medicinal harvesting is more than a practice—it's a commitment to living in sync with nature's rhythms. By understanding how the seasons affect plant growth and potency, you can optimize your medicinal plant harvests, ensuring that you gather the most efficacious herbs at their peak.

Spring Renewal

As the frost recedes and the earth thaws, nature awakens with a burst of life. Spring is a time of renewal, and many medicinal plants begin their cycle of growth during this season. For the herbal prepper, this is a prime time to collect leafy greens such as nettles, chickweed, and dandelion. These plants are at their nutritional and medicinal peak in the spring when their new growth contains high concentrations of vitamins and minerals.

In the cool, damp mornings of early spring, look for young nettles before they flower, as they are less stringy and their histamine content is lower. Harvesting nettles at this time ensures a supply of leaves that are ideal for teas and tinctures aimed at detoxification and boosting immune health. Similarly, harvesting the tender leaves of dandelion provides a diuretic benefit that supports liver and kidney function, perfect for a springtime cleanse.

Summer's Abundance

Summer brings warmth and a profusion of blooming medicinal plants. This is the season to focus on collecting flowering tops and aromatic leaves. Plants like chamomile, lavender, and yarrow should be harvested on dry, sunny days when they are fully open and rich in essential oils, which are potentiated by the intense summer sun.

Chamomile flowers picked at this time are perfect for soothing teas that calm the digestive system and help reduce anxiety and insomnia. Lavender, harvested at peak bloom, can be used to create calming tinctures and oils that also serve as effective remedies for skin irritations and burns. The robust energy of summer imbues these plants with vibrant vitality, making their medicinal properties especially powerful.

Autumn's Harvest

As the days begin to shorten and the temperatures drop, autumn signals the time to collect roots and barks, which are now densely packed with nutrients and medicinal compounds. This is when perennial plants like echinacea, valerian, and burdock send their energy and resources back down into their roots in preparation for winter.

Harvesting echinacea roots in the fall can maximize the concentration of immune-boosting alkamides, which are essential for making tinctures that ward off winter colds. Valerian roots, too, are best dug up in the fall when they are full of valerenic acid, effective for promoting sleep and reducing anxiety. This time of year, with its focus on the earthier parts of plants, calls for a deep dive into the soil, connecting you physically and spiritually to the land.

Winter's Rest

Winter might seem like a time to pause, but it's an ideal period for planning and preparation. While the ground is frozen and the garden is quiet, spend time strategizing your harvests for the upcoming year. It's also a period for processing and preserving the bounty collected throughout other seasons. Drying, making tinctures, and creating salves and balms are all perfect winter activities that set the foundation for year-round herbal use.

Additionally, winter is the time for wild harvesting evergreens like pine, fir, and spruce, whose needles are rich in vitamin C and can be used to make invigorating teas that ward off winter ailments. Harvesting these in the cold months, when few other plants are available, provides a unique opportunity to maintain a connection with nature and sustain your herbal practice throughout the year.

Understanding Plant Signals

Each plant species has its own specific signs and signals that indicate the optimal time for harvesting. Learning these signs requires observation and experience. For instance, certain herbs may exude a stronger aroma at their medicinal peak, while others might display a particular color or form of their leaves and flowers. The key to successful seasonal harvesting is not just knowing these signs, but also being attuned to the subtle changes in the environment that affect plant growth. As you develop a rhythm with the seasons, your herbal medicine chest will grow not only in size but in potency. The art of seasonal harvesting is not merely about collecting plants; it's about embracing a lifestyle that respects and enhances your connection to the natural world, ensuring that you and your loved ones have access to the best possible natural health resources. This approach not only enriches your life but also ensures that the natural ecosystems you rely on are protected and sustained, allowing you to continue harvesting year after year.

As we journey deeper into the world of natural medicine, understanding the foundational principles of herbal medicine is essential. This chapter serves as your guide to the underlying scientific and philosophical elements that make herbalism a powerful tool for health and well-being. Here, we delve into how plants interact with the body to promote healing, balance, and resilience.

Herbal medicine is not just about using plants as substitutes for pharmaceuticals; it's about embracing a holistic approach to health that considers the physical, mental, and environmental factors influencing our well-being. We will explore how to prepare your body to receive these natural remedies, ensuring that the benefits extend beyond the surface symptoms to foster deeper, lasting health.

Through this exploration, you will learn how to seamlessly integrate herbal medicine into your daily life, making it a natural extension of your everyday practices. This isn't merely about having a set of recipes but about fostering a lifestyle that aligns with the rhythms of nature and the wisdom of our ancestors. Prepare to see your kitchen, your garden, and even your local wild spaces as parts of a living pharmacy that you are equipped to utilize with confidence and respect.

1. The Science of Herbalism

Herbalism, often viewed through a mystical lens, is deeply rooted in the sciences of botany, chemistry, and medicine. It bridges traditional knowledge with modern scientific inquiry, making it a comprehensive discipline that invites both respect and rigorous study. At its core, herbalism is the science and art of using plants for medicinal purposes, a practice that has evolved over millennia, supported by ongoing research and clinical studies.

Understanding the science behind herbalism begins with phytochemistry, the study of chemicals derived from plants. Plants produce a wide range of chemical compounds known as phytochemicals, which serve various functions, such as protecting the plant from pests and diseases, aiding in reproduction, and more. In human use, these phytochemicals interact with the body's biological systems, providing therapeutic effects. For example, the salicylic acid found in willow bark is a pain reliever and anti-inflammatory agent, famously synthesized into aspirin.

Each plant contains a unique set of phytochemicals, which can be isolated and studied for their effects on human health. Alkaloids, flavonoids, terpenes, and saponins are just a few examples of these compounds, each having distinct properties and health benefits. Alkaloids, for instance, are known for their powerful effects on the nervous system, while flavonoids are celebrated for their antioxidant properties.

The process of extracting these compounds is as important as the compounds themselves. Various methods such as infusion, decoction, tincturing, and pressing are used to draw out the active ingredients from the plant material. The choice of extraction method depends on the specific plant and the desired compounds. For example, volatile oils are best captured through steam distillation, while tincturing in alcohol can preserve a broader spectrum of plant constituents over an extended period.

Beyond extraction, the formulation of herbal remedies requires an understanding of how different herbs interact with each other and with the human body. This knowledge is partly derived from traditional uses but is increasingly being validated and expanded by scientific research. Studies may focus on the efficacy of a single herb or the synergistic effects of an herbal blend, providing a richer understanding of how plant compounds influence health.

Clinical trials and pharmacological studies play crucial roles in modern herbalism. They provide empirical data to support traditional claims and help herbalists understand the mechanisms by which plant compounds act within the body. For example, numerous studies have validated the use of St. John's Wort in treating mild to moderate depression, positioning it as a viable alternative to synthetic antidepressants for some patients. Safety is a paramount concern in the practice of herbalism, just as it is in conventional medicine.

Understanding the potential side effects, contraindications, and interactions of herbal remedies with drugs is crucial. This is where the science of pharmacokinetics and pharmacodynamics comes into play, as it involves studying how substances are absorbed, distributed, metabolized, and excreted by the body.

Herbalism also embraces a holistic approach to health, considering the individual's entire well-being rather than just focusing on suppressing symptoms. This philosophy aligns with many traditional healing systems, which view health as a balance of physical, emotional, mental, and sometimes spiritual elements. In this context, herbs are selected not just for their active ingredients but for their overall impact on an individual's health, taking into account their unique constitution and the underlying causes of their condition.

Education and communication are key aspects of practicing herbalism responsibly. As practitioners and enthusiasts, our role extends beyond personal or clinical use to advocating for informed, safe, and ethical use of herbs. This involves staying updated with the latest research, adhering to regulatory standards, and educating the public about the benefits and limitations of herbal medicine.

In integrating science with tradition, herbalism offers a dynamic and evolving path to health that honors our natural connections to the earth while benefiting from the rigorous testing and analysis of modern science. It's a field where every plant tells a story, every remedy has a history, and every practice is underpinned by a complex array of biological activities that are just beginning to be fully understood.

2. Preparing Your Body for Herbal Remedies

Integrating herbal remedies into your wellness regimen isn't merely a matter of selecting and using herbs. It's equally about preparing your body to effectively absorb and utilize these natural substances, ensuring they contribute positively to your health. This process of preparation involves nurturing your body's own systems to optimize its responsiveness, a practice that is as much about lifestyle choices as it is about specific herbal interventions.

To truly harness the power of herbs, begin by understanding the concept of holistic health, which emphasizes the interconnection between the physical, mental, and emotional aspects of well-being. Herbs work best in a body that is balanced and ready to receive their benefits. Therefore, preparing your body involves fostering a foundation of good health through nutrition, hydration, exercise, and stress management.

Nutrition plays a pivotal role in this preparation. A diet rich in whole foods provides the essential nutrients that support all bodily functions, including detoxification, healing, and regeneration.

Foods that are particularly supportive include leafy greens, fruits, nuts, seeds, and whole grains, which offer a rich array of vitamins, minerals, antioxidants, and fibers. These nutrients help maintain a healthy gut microbiome, which is crucial for immune function and the absorption of herbal compounds. Introducing fermented foods can further enhance gut health, preparing the body to utilize herbs effectively.

Hydration is another cornerstone. Water is essential for every cellular function and helps the body to process and excrete the active compounds in herbs. Maintaining optimal hydration ensures that the kidneys and liver, the primary organs involved in detoxification and metabolism of substances, function efficiently. This is particularly important when using diuretic herbs or those that stimulate the liver.

Exercise, while often touted for its cardiovascular benefits, also enhances circulation and detoxification. Regular physical activity helps pump blood through the body, facilitating the spread of nutrients and the removal of wastes. This improved circulation means that the beneficial compounds in herbal remedies can reach their targets more effectively. Additionally, exercise increases your respiratory rate, aiding the lungs in expelling waste products, which can be crucial when using respiratory herbs.

Stress management is crucial in preparing your body for herbal remedies. Chronic stress can undermine health in numerous ways, from disrupting hormonal balance to weakening the immune system. Herbs often work not just on the physical symptoms but also on the underlying stress factors. Techniques such as meditation, yoga, and deep breathing exercises can help manage stress, thus creating a more receptive environment for herbal treatments.

Beyond these foundational lifestyle adjustments, detoxifying the body is a significant step in preparation. The goal here is not the often misinterpreted 'cleansing' fads, but a reasoned approach to reducing the load of toxins and stressors that impede health. This includes minimizing exposure to synthetic chemicals and environmental toxins in foods, personal care products, and the home environment. Incorporating herbs with detoxifying properties, such as milk thistle for the liver or dandelion root, which supports both liver and kidneys, can be particularly beneficial when done under the guidance of a knowledgeable herbalist.

Equally important is supporting the organs of elimination, such as the liver, kidneys, and colon, to ensure they are functioning optimally before beginning any regimen that includes potent medicinal herbs. This might involve using gentle supportive herbs, such as burdock root or yellow dock, which gently enhance the natural detoxification processes without overburdening the body. Sleep, often overlooked, is essential for healing and restoration. Ensuring you get adequate and quality sleep is crucial when preparing for and using herbal remedies. Many herbs, such as chamomile or valerian, support sleep and can be integrated into your nightly routine to enhance sleep quality, thereby supporting the body's natural healing processes.

Lastly, it is important to approach herbal medicine with mindfulness and intention. Being mindful of the effects herbs have on your body and adjusting usage based on your observations can lead to more personalized and effective herbal treatment. This mindfulness extends to recognizing when herbal remedies are beneficial and when they might need to be adjusted or ceased.

By nurturing your body through these comprehensive approaches, you create an environment where herbal remedies can work most effectively. This preparation does not merely enhance the effects of herbs but also contributes to a broader, sustainable approach to health that reduces reliance on conventional medicines and fosters long-term well-being.

3. Integrating Herbal Medicine into Daily Life

Incorporating herbal medicine into your daily life is a profound step towards embracing a holistic approach to health. It's about more than merely taking a remedy when you feel ill; it's about weaving the power of plants into your everyday routines, creating a lifestyle that naturally promotes wellness and balance.

The integration of herbal medicine begins with a simple, yet pivotal, step: understanding the herbs themselves. Knowing which herbs are suited for which conditions, how they can be prepared, and the best times to use them is foundational. This knowledge allows you to make informed decisions about the herbs that will most benefit your specific health needs and lifestyle.

Start with familiarizing yourself with a few key herbs that address common ailments and conditions prevalent in modern life. For example, chamomile and lavender are renowned for their calming effects and can be easily incorporated into bedtime routines to enhance sleep. Similarly, ginger and peppermint are excellent for digestive health and can be consumed as teas after meals to aid digestion.

Creating herbal rituals is an effective way to integrate these plants into your daily routine. Morning may involve a tonic of lemon, honey, and ginger to awaken the body and stimulate the digestive system, setting a vibrant tone for the day. Throughout the day, switching from coffee to green tea can reduce caffeine intake while providing antioxidant benefits.

In the kitchen, culinary herbs not only enhance flavor but also offer health benefits. Rosemary, thyme, and basil can be grown on a kitchen windowsill and added fresh to dishes, bridging the gap between food and medicine. Herbs such as turmeric and cinnamon can be incorporated into meals not just for their flavor, but for their anti-inflammatory and antioxidant properties. Personal care is another area where herbs can play a significant role. Skin care products can be enriched with herbs like calendula and aloe vera, known for their soothing and healing properties. Homemade or artisanal herbal soaps, shampoos, and lotions can turn routine hygiene into an act of self-care that nurtures the body with natural ingredients.

For those managing chronic conditions, integrating specific herbs into your management plan can be beneficial. However, this should always be done in consultation with healthcare providers to ensure safety, particularly regarding potential interactions with prescribed medications. Herbs like hawthorn for heart health or cinnamon for blood sugar regulation can complement conventional treatments under proper guidance.

The seasonal use of herbs is another facet of integration. Just as foods are consumed seasonally, so too can herbs be used in a way that aligns with the body's changing needs throughout the year. Spring might focus on detoxifying herbs like nettle and dandelion, summer could lean on cooling herbs like peppermint, while fall and winter would benefit from immune-boosting herbs like elderberry and echinacea.

Involving the family in herbal practices can also deepen the integration into daily life. Teaching children about the herbs growing in the garden, their uses, and how to prepare simple remedies like lemon balm tea for a soothing drink can be both educational and empowering. It encourages a family culture of wellness and respect for nature's gifts.

Finally, embracing the community aspect of herbalism can further solidify its role in your daily life. Joining or forming herbal study groups, attending workshops, and participating in community gardens can expand your knowledge and appreciation of herbal medicine. These communal activities offer support and exchange of ideas, making herbal practices more enjoyable and sustainable.

Integrating herbal medicine into daily life is not a one-time event but a gradual, ongoing process of learning, experiencing, and adjusting. It's about building a relationship with the natural world that is nurturing, sustaining, and, ultimately, healing. As you incorporate these practices into your daily routines, you'll find that herbal medicine doesn't just address specific ailments—it enhances overall well-being and connects you more deeply to the natural rhythms of life.

4. Ethical Considerations and Sustainability in Herbal Practice

Ethical considerations and sustainability in herbal practice are foundational elements that ensure the longevity of herbalism not just as a craft, but as a vital form of ecological stewardship. As we delve deeper into the realm of herbal medicine, it is crucial to foster a relationship with the earth that is based on respect, sustainability, and a deep understanding of the impact our actions have on the natural world.

Ethical harvesting is about more than just choosing the right plants at the right time—it's about harvesting in a way that maintains and even enhances the health and abundance of plant populations for future generations. This involves knowing how much to harvest, which parts of the plant to take, and ensuring that enough remains for the plant to continue its life cycle effectively. It also means recognizing and avoiding plants that are endangered or under threat from overharvesting. By practicing careful, informed harvesting, herbalists can help to sustain plant populations and the ecosystems in which they thrive.

Growing your own medicinal plants is a profound way to engage with the plant world. It allows for a greater control over the supply chain, from seed to remedy, and ensures that plants are grown in a sustainable manner. This includes using organic methods that do not rely on chemical pesticides or fertilizers that can harm the environment. It also means using water responsibly and creating a garden ecosystem that supports biodiversity, including insects and other wildlife, which play a crucial role in the health of the garden.

Sustainable cultivation also involves selecting appropriate plants for the local climate and soil conditions, which requires less water, fewer supplements, and adapts more harmoniously with the local environment. Furthermore, cultivating native plants often requires less effort in terms of both water and soil management, as these plants are naturally suited to thrive in their indigenous settings.

When cultivation is not possible, purchasing herbs from responsible sources becomes paramount. Opting for suppliers who practice fair trade can ensure that those who grow and collect the herbs are paid fairly and work under good conditions. This not only supports local economies but also encourages the sustainable production of herbal products. Supporting local economies further reduces the carbon footprint associated with transporting herbs across great distances, thus contributing to a more sustainable practice of herbal medicine.

Engaging in or supporting conservation efforts can also be a part of sustainable herbal practice. This can involve participating in local and global efforts to preserve natural habitats and to educate the public about the importance of conserving both plant species and their natural environments. Community involvement can amplify these efforts, creating a network of knowledgeable individuals who respect and protect their local environments.

Herbalists can contribute by leading workshops on sustainable harvesting and cultivation, participating in community garden projects, and sharing their knowledge about the medicinal value of local plants. By fostering a community that values and understands the importance of sustainable practices, herbalists can help ensure that herbal medicine remains a viable and responsible choice for future generations.

Reducing one's carbon footprint is another key aspect of sustainable herbal practice. This includes minimizing the use of non-renewable resources in the preparation, packaging, and distribution of herbal products. For example, using glass or biodegradable packaging instead of plastic, and minimizing waste in all stages of the herbal process are steps that help align herbal practice with ecological values.

As climate change continues to affect plant populations and ecosystems, herbalists must adapt their practices accordingly. This might involve altering planting and harvesting schedules, using water conservation techniques, and selecting plant varieties that are more resilient to changes in climate. By staying informed about climate science and being proactive in adaptive practices, herbalists can help their practices evolve in a way that respects and responds to the changing environment.

Ultimately, ethical considerations and sustainability in herbal medicine are about much more than just the individual practice of collecting and using plants—it's about contributing to a global ethos of environmental stewardship. Herbalists have a unique opportunity to lead by example, showing how traditional practices can be adapted to modern ecological challenges in ways that are respectful, sustainable, and forward-thinking. By embedding these principles into every aspect of herbal practice, we ensure that our relationship with the natural world is one of mutual respect and mutual benefit, preserving the vitality and viability of herbal medicine for generations to come.

Every home should have a first aid kit, but what about one that harnesses the natural healing power of herbs? Building an herbal first aid kit equips you not only to respond to everyday ailments but also to engage actively with your own health care using the gentle yet potent power of nature. This chapter guides you through assembling a comprehensive herbal toolkit tailored for a variety of common health scenarios—from cuts and scrapes to digestive upset and stress relief.

Think of your herbal first aid kit as your go-to resource for quick, effective responses when health issues arise. Just as you might reach for a bandage or an ice pack, so too will you turn to your cache of chamomile, lavender, or echinacea. But beyond mere reaction, this kit represents your commitment to proactive well-being, blending traditional knowledge with practical application, ensuring you and your family are supported by nature's bounty at every turn.

In these pages, you'll discover how to select, prepare, and utilize herbs in ways that are both practical and meaningful, ensuring that your herbal first aid kit becomes an indispensable part of your health care routine, ready at a moment's notice to soothe, heal, and restore.

1. Essential Herbs and Their Uses

Creating an herbal first aid kit starts with a selection of essential herbs that address a broad range of common ailments. These herbs form the backbone of your kit, providing natural remedies for everything from skin irritations and wounds to digestive disturbances and stress-related symptoms. By understanding the properties and uses of these essential herbs, you can handle many minor health issues safely and effectively at home.

Calendula (Calendula officinalis), with its vibrant golden blooms, is a must-have for any herbal first aid kit. Renowned for its anti-inflammatory and antimicrobial properties, calendula is excellent for treating cuts, scrapes, burns, and rashes. It can be applied as a salve or cream to soothe inflamed skin and promote healing.

Chamomile (Matricaria recutita) is another indispensable herb, particularly known for its calming effects. It is ideal for treating insomnia, anxiety, and stress, but its benefits don't stop there. Chamomile tea can soothe the digestive system, relieve menstrual cramps, and reduce inflammation. A cooled chamomile tea bag is also a gentle remedy for tired, irritated eyes.

Peppermint (Mentha piperita) is highly valued for its digestive benefits. Peppermint tea is a well-known remedy for nausea, indigestion, and gas. Its cooling properties make it useful in balms for relieving headaches when applied to the temples or the back of the neck.

Lavender (Lavandula angustifolia) is celebrated for its soothing scent and its ability to alleviate anxiety, insomnia, and stress. Additionally, lavender oil can be used to treat burns, cuts, and stings by reducing pain, preventing infection, and supporting rapid healing.

Echinacea (Echinacea spp.) is your go-to herb for immune support. Beginning to take echinacea at the onset of a cold or flu can help reduce the severity and duration of these illnesses. It can also be applied topically as a tincture or infused oil to cleanse wounds and promote healing.

Ginger (Zingiber officinale), with its warm, spicy flavor, is a powerful herb for gastrointestinal relief. It effectively combats nausea, motion sickness, and morning sickness. Ginger can also be used to reduce inflammation and is particularly soothing in the form of tea or a hot compress for achy muscles and joints.

Arnica (Arnica montana) should be included for its ability to treat bruises, sprains, and muscle soreness. Applied as a cream or gel (not taken internally), arnica can significantly reduce swelling and speed up recovery from physical injuries.

Tea Tree Oil (Melaleuca alternifolia), while not an herb in the traditional sense, is an essential inclusion for its potent antiseptic properties. It can be used to treat a variety of skin issues, including acne, fungal infections, and dandruff. Tea tree oil must be diluted before application to avoid skin irritation.

Aloe Vera (Aloe barbadensis miller) is unparalleled for skin care. Its gel soothes sunburns, cuts, and other skin irritations with immediate cooling relief. Keeping a fresh aloe vera plant in the kitchen is not only practical for quick burn relief but also serves as a constant reminder of the healing power of plants.

Each of these herbs can be prepared in various forms depending on their use. Tinctures, teas, salves, and oils are common preparations that make the properties of the herbs more accessible and convenient to use in everyday situations. Creating these preparations in advance and storing them in your first aid kit means you're always prepared to handle minor medical issues naturally. In addition to the practical applications, cultivating a relationship with each herb in your kit enhances your understanding and appreciation of their uses. Experimenting with growing your own herbs, preparing remedies, and using them in real-life situations builds confidence and proficiency in herbal medicine. This hands-on approach not only ensures that you are prepared to use your first aid kit effectively but also deepens your connection to the natural world.

Assembling an herbal first aid kit isn't just about being prepared for emergencies—it's about embracing a lifestyle that values the gentle strength of nature and its capacity to heal. This kit becomes a symbol of self-sufficiency and a testament to the power of natural remedies, ready to support your health at a moment's notice.

2. Storage and Preservation Techniques

Proper storage and preservation of herbal remedies are crucial for maintaining their potency and effectiveness. When building an herbal first aid kit, knowing how to preserve your herbs and preparations ensures that they are both safe and beneficial at the time of use. Each herb and its various forms, from dried leaves to essential oils, require specific conditions to preserve their medicinal qualities.

Drying Herbs is the most traditional method of preserving their properties. The key to drying herbs effectively is to ensure they are free of moisture to prevent mold and decay. Hang bunches of fresh herbs upside down in a warm, dry, and well-ventilated area away from direct sunlight. Once the herbs are completely dry, which may take several days to a few weeks depending on the herb and the environment, gently strip the leaves or flowers from the stems and store them in airtight containers. Glass jars with tight-fitting lids are ideal as they do not impart any flavors and prevent air from entering.

Storing Dried Herbs requires attention to detail to maintain their therapeutic properties. Keep your jars in a cool, dark place—light and heat can degrade the active compounds in dried herbs. Label each container with the herb's name and the date of drying; most dried herbs retain their potency for up to a year if stored correctly.

Tinctures are another popular form for storing herbs in your kit. They are prepared by macerating (soaking) herbs in alcohol, which extracts and preserves their active ingredients. To make a tincture, fill a jar one-third to one-half with dried herbs, then pour in enough vodka, rum, or brandy to completely cover the herbs. Seal the jar and store it in a cool, dark place, shaking it daily for the first two weeks. After four to six weeks, strain the liquid through a cheesecloth and transfer it to amber dropper bottles for easy use. Alcohol-based tinctures can last for several years and are an effective way to preserve the potency of herbs.

Herbal Oils involve infusing herbs in a carrier oil to extract their active compounds. Commonly used oils include olive oil, coconut oil, or almond oil due to their stability and mild scent. The infusion process can be done using a double boiler method where herbs and oil are gently heated over low heat for several hours, or by letting the mixture sit in a warm, sunny spot for several weeks. Once strained, store herbal oils in dark glass bottles in a cool, dark place. Due to their oil content, they are more prone to rancidity than tinctures and typically last for about six months to a year.

Salves and Balms are convenient for topical application and can be made by thickening herbal oils with beeswax. To make a salve, gently heat the infused oil and slowly melt beeswax into the oil until the desired consistency is achieved. Pour the mixture into small tins or jars and let it solidify. Stored away from heat and light, salves can last up to a year.

Powders are made by grinding dried herbs into a fine consistency. Store powders in airtight containers in a dry place, and they can last up to six months. Herbal powders are versatile and can be used to quickly make capsules or mixed into teas and foods.

When preserving herbal preparations, **labeling** is essential. Always label your containers with the herb name, type of preparation, concentration if applicable, and the date of preparation. This practice not only helps in identifying the contents but also in monitoring their shelf life and ensuring they are used at their peak effectiveness.

For those who frequently travel or want to ensure they have remedies on hand at all times, **portable versions** of your herbal first aid kit can be created. Smaller bottles for tinctures, mini-salve tins, and individual packets of herbal teas are convenient and easy to carry.

Maintaining the integrity of your herbal remedies through proper storage and preservation techniques is key to ensuring that your first aid kit is always ready to provide natural, effective care. This attention to detail not only maximizes the life span of your preparations but also enhances your overall wellness strategy, empowering you with readiness and confidence in handling health needs naturally.

3. Herbal Remedies for Common Ailments

An herbal first aid kit is your gateway to natural and effective remedies for managing common ailments. It's a personalized medicine cabinet that allows you to respond swiftly to everyday health issues with preparations you trust. Knowing which herbs to use and how to use them for various common ailments can transform your approach to health care, making it more natural, informed, and proactive.

For skin injuries such as cuts and scrapes, **calendula** and **lavender** are invaluable. Calendula, applied as a salve or gel, can speed up healing and reduce inflammation thanks to its antimicrobial and healing properties. Lavender essential oil, diluted in a carrier oil, can be gently dabbed on minor cuts to cleanse the wound and promote healing due to its antibacterial and soothing effects. For minor burns, **aloe vera** stands out as a go-to remedy. The gel inside the aloe vera leaf is naturally cooling and soothing, providing immediate relief while its anti-inflammatory properties help reduce swelling and speed up healing. For extra healing power, combine aloe vera gel with a few drops of lavender essential oil before applying it to the burn.

Plantain (Plantago major), a common leafy green found in many backyards, is highly effective against the itching and inflammation of insect bites and stings. Fresh plantain leaves can be crushed or chewed and applied directly to the bite. Alternatively, a salve made from infused plantain oil can be applied to soothe skin and reduce irritation.

Peppermint oil is a well-documented remedy for tension headaches. Applying diluted peppermint oil to the temples or the back of the neck can provide relief from headache pain due to its cooling properties and its ability to promote blood flow. **Ginger** tea can also alleviate headaches, especially those related to digestive issues, by reducing inflammation and soothing nausea.

For nausea, indigestion, and general gastrointestinal discomfort, **ginger** and **peppermint** are powerful allies. Ginger tea can soothe the stomach and reduce nausea, while peppermint tea helps relieve symptoms of indigestion and gas. For a quick remedy, capsules containing dried ginger or peppermint oil can be effective.

At the first sign of a cold, **echinacea** tincture can help reduce the severity and duration of symptoms. It boosts the immune system and can be taken at the onset of symptoms. **Elderberry syrup** is another excellent remedy for both prevention and treatment of colds and flu, known for its antiviral properties.

Thyme is highly effective for sore throats due to its antibacterial and antiviral properties. A tea made from thyme can be gargled to relieve throat pain and combat infections. **Sage** tea, similarly, can be used as a gargle and is particularly soothing for inflamed mucous membranes.

Chamomile tea is renowned for its calming effects, making it an ideal choice for reducing stress and aiding relaxation. For those who experience anxiety, a tincture of **lemon balm** can be taken, as it acts as a mild sedative, helping to calm nerves and improve mood.

For help with sleep, **valerian root** and **hops** are powerful herbs known for their sedative properties. A tea or tincture taken before bedtime can help facilitate a quicker and more restful sleep. Combining these with lavender, either in a diffuser or as a pillow spray, can enhance the sleep-inducing effects.

For those suffering from joint pain or muscle aches, **arnica cream** is excellent for topical application, helping to reduce pain and swelling. Infused oils of **st. John's wort** or **comfrey** can also be used to massage sore muscles and joints, providing anti-inflammatory benefits and soothing relief.

Creating remedies for these common ailments involves more than just knowing which herbs to use; it's about understanding how to prepare and apply these herbs effectively. Whether you are brewing a tea, compounding a tincture, or mixing a salve, the key to successful treatment lies in the quality of your ingredients and the care with which you prepare and store them.

By integrating these herbal remedies into your first aid kit, you equip yourself with the tools needed to manage health naturally and safely. This approach not only empowers you to take charge of your health but also deepens your connection to the natural world, offering a fulfilling way to care for yourself and your loved ones with the gentle power of plants.

4. Personalizing Your Herbal First Aid Kit

Personalizing your herbal first aid kit is a dynamic process that significantly enhances its utility, ensuring that you have precisely what you need, when you need it. By tailoring the contents of your kit to suit personal health profiles, lifestyle choices, and specific environmental needs, you can ensure that your preparedness is not only thorough but also exceptionally practical.

To start personalizing your herbal first aid kit, take a comprehensive look at the health trends and recurring ailments in your household. For instance, if seasonal allergies are a frequent disturbance, including herbs like nettle for its antihistamine properties or butterbur for reducing inflammation can be highly beneficial. For households dealing with chronic issues such as arthritis or digestive problems, stocking up on turmeric for its anti-inflammatory properties and ginger for its gastrointestinal benefits is wise.

The activities that dominate your family's lifestyle should significantly influence the contents of your herbal first aid kit. If your family is active and spends a lot of time outdoors, you'll need to be prepared for cuts, bruises, insect bites, and perhaps sunburns. Here, aloe vera for sunburns, plantain for its soothing properties on insect bites and cuts, and arnica for bruises would be essential. On the other hand, if your family leads a more sedentary indoor lifestyle, your kit might focus more on remedies like peppermint for headaches or chamomile for stress and anxiety.

The environment you live in plays a crucial role in determining what goes into your herbal first aid kit. For those in rural or wooded areas, adding tick and insect repellents such as lemon eucalyptus oil or tea tree oil can be a priority. In contrast, urban dwellers might emphasize pollution-related ailments like respiratory issues, where mullein or licorice root could be beneficial for soothing the respiratory tract.

Adapting your kit with the changing seasons is another critical aspect of personalization. During flu and cold season, ensure your kit is stocked with elderberry syrup, echinacea, and thyme, all of which bolster the immune system and fight viruses. In contrast, summer might call for more calendula cream for minor cuts and scrapes that are common with outdoor activities, and witch hazel for cooling skin irritations.

Consider the age range of your family members when assembling your kit. For children, milder and safer herbs like chamomile (for sleep or stomach upset) and lavender (for minor burns or sleep) are crucial. For elderly family members who may manage chronic conditions, herbs that support heart health and cognitive function, such as hawthorn and ginkgo, might be necessary additions.

If your family travels frequently, consider a portable version of your herbal first aid kit that can easily go with you. This travel kit should include remedies that address common travel-related issues such as motion sickness, for which ginger capsules can be effective, or aloe vera gel for quick relief from sunburns.

Reflect on past health incidents that could have been managed more effectively if specific remedies had been available. This reflection can guide you to include certain herbs that you might not have considered previously. For example, if someone in your family experienced food poisoning and you found that activated charcoal or peppermint helped, these should find a permanent place in your kit.

For those new to herbal medicine or those with complex health conditions, consulting with a professional herbalist when personalizing your kit can provide invaluable insights. They can offer advice tailored to your specific health needs and help identify any potential interactions with conventional medications being taken.

Finally, the process of personalizing your herbal first aid kit is ongoing. As your family grows and changes, so too should your kit. Regularly review and update the kit to adapt to any new health conditions, changes in lifestyle, or even advancements in herbal medicine knowledge.

By taking the time to personalize your herbal first aid kit, you're not just preparing for emergencies—you're investing in a form of health empowerment. This proactive approach ensures that when medical issues arise, you are ready with effective, natural remedies that align closely with your family's specific health needs and environmental conditions.

Mastering the art of herbal preparations is a transformative journey that enhances your connection to nature and deepens your understanding of personal health. This chapter is your guide to the hands-on process of crafting your own herbal remedies—from tinctures and extracts to salves and teas. Each preparation method not only preserves the therapeutic properties of plants but also optimizes their effectiveness for healing and wellness.

As you learn to blend, infuse, decoct, and macerate, you will discover the profound satisfaction that comes from creating something both beautiful and beneficial. Whether it's concocting a soothing balm from calendula, brewing a potent digestive tea from peppermint, or extracting the immune-boosting essence of echinacea, each recipe and technique will equip you with practical skills that can be applied in everyday situations.

This chapter isn't just a set of instructions; it's an invitation to engage actively with the natural world, to experiment with the gifts it offers, and to weave these gifts into the fabric of daily life. Through the art of herbal preparations, you will learn to harness the power of plants in ways that nurture your body, soothe your mind, and elevate your spirit.

1. Making Tinctures and Extracts

Tinctures and extracts stand as pillars within the world of herbal remedies, offering a powerful means to harness and preserve the medicinal properties of herbs. Making tinctures and extracts not only ensures a long shelf life for your herbal preparations but also provides a potent, easy-to-use form of herbal medicine.

Tinctures are alcohol-based extracts that utilize ethanol to pull out the active compounds from plants. The alcohol acts as a solvent that extracts a wide range of phytochemicals, including those that are not water-soluble, making tinctures one of the most effective means of preserving the medicinal qualities of herbs.

Start with choosing high-quality, dried herbs. Fresh herbs can also be used, but their water content can dilute the tincture, potentially leading to spoilage. Select herbs known for their efficacy in addressing specific conditions or for general health benefits—such as echinacea for immune support, valerian root for sleep, or dandelion for liver health.

Ethanol, typically sourced as high-proof alcohol like vodka or brandy, is ideal for making tinctures. The alcohol concentration should be at least 40% to ensure effective extraction and preservation of the plant's properties. For those avoiding alcohol, glycerin or vinegar can be alternatives, though they may not extract a wide range of compounds as effectively.

Preparing the Tincture

1. **Filling the Jar**: Place your chosen herbs in a clean glass jar, filling it one-half to two-thirds full. The more space the herbs take up, the stronger your tincture will be.

2. **Adding Alcohol**: Pour the alcohol over the herbs until they are completely submerged. Ensure there is about a two-inch margin of alcohol above the herbs to allow them to expand.

3. **Sealing and Labeling**: Close the jar tightly and label it with the date and the herbs used. This helps in tracking the steeping time and identifying the tincture later.

4. **Steeping**: Store the jar in a cool, dark place for four to six weeks. Shake the jar daily to help the alcohol better extract the herbal constituents.

Once steeping is complete, strain the liquid through cheesecloth or a fine mesh strainer into another clean glass jar. Compress the herbs to squeeze out as much liquid as possible. Transfer the strained tincture into dark glass dropper bottles for easy use. Stored properly, tinctures can last up to several years.

While similar to tinctures, extracts often involve other solvents like water, glycerin, or oil to draw out the active components of herbs. Water-based extracts, or decoctions, are typically used for hard, woody substances like roots or bark.

Making a Decoction

1. **Preparing the Herbs**: Chop the dried roots, bark, or berries finely to increase the surface area for extraction.

2. **Boiling**: Place the herbs in a pot and cover them with water. Bring to a boil, then reduce to a simmer.

3. **Simmering**: Allow the mixture to simmer gently for about 20 to 30 minutes. Keep the pot covered to prevent the evaporation of water and volatile compounds.

4. **Cooling and Straining**: Remove from heat and let it cool. Strain the decoction through a fine mesh, squeezing the herbs to extract the liquid fully.

5. **Storage**: Store the decoction in a clean glass bottle in the refrigerator for up to a week. For longer storage, decoctions can be frozen into ice cubes and thawed as needed.

Glycerin is a sweet, syrupy substance that works well for making non-alcoholic extracts, especially for children. Vinegar, with its acidic nature, can extract different compounds beneficial for health but typically has a shorter shelf life and distinct taste.

Practical Tips

- **Herb Quality**: Always use the best quality herbs you can find—organic and sustainably sourced are preferable.

- **Labeling**: Comprehensive labeling on each jar and bottle will ensure you remember which tincture is which and when it was made.

- **Testing Potency**: It's wise to test the potency of your tinctures and extracts. Start with small doses to ensure their effectiveness and your tolerance.

Through the meticulous crafting of tinctures and extracts, you delve into a tradition of herbal medicine that is both ancient and profoundly relevant. These preparations not only provide a compact, convenient way to utilize the healing power of plants but also invite a deeper connection to the natural world, enhancing your well-being and broadening your self-care toolkit.

2. Crafting Salves and Balms

Crafting salves and balms is a deeply satisfying aspect of herbal medicine, blending the art of formulation with the practicality of creating versatile, healing products. These preparations are ideal for treating a wide array of skin ailments, from dry skin and chapped lips to burns, wounds, and irritations. Unlike creams and lotions, salves and balms are typically water-free, relying on the synergy of oils and waxes to create protective barriers on the skin while delivering therapeutic herbs directly to the areas where they are most needed. The base for any salve or balm generally consists of three primary components: a carrier oil, beeswax, and herbal extracts. The carrier oil serves as the medium that absorbs the essence of the herbs. Common choices include olive oil, coconut oil, almond oil, or jojoba oil, each bringing its own therapeutic properties as well as a unique texture to the final product.

The first step in crafting a salve or balm is to infuse your chosen carrier oil with herbs. This can be done using the double boiler method, where herbs and oil are gently heated over low heat to avoid burning the oil while releasing the active compounds from the herbs. Alternatively, for those who prefer a slower, more traditional approach, the solar infusion method allows the sun's warmth to naturally infuse the oil over three to four weeks.

1. **Double Boiler Method**: Place dried herbs and carrier oil in a double boiler, ensuring the herbs are fully submerged. Heat the mixture over low heat for two to three hours, stirring occasionally.

2. **Solar Infusion Method**: Fill a clean, dry jar with dried herbs and cover them completely with carrier oil. Seal the jar and place it in a sunny spot for three to four weeks, shaking daily.

After infusion, strain the oil through a cheesecloth, squeezing out as much oil as possible. This infused oil is now ready to be transformed into a salve or balm.

The next step is to determine the desired consistency of your product. For a firmer balm, a higher ratio of beeswax to oil is needed, whereas salves generally require less beeswax to maintain a softer texture.

1. **Measuring Beeswax**: As a general rule, start with a ratio of one part beeswax to eight parts oil for a soft salve. For balms, increase the beeswax to achieve a stiffer product.

2. **Melting the Beeswax**: Combine the beeswax with your infused oil in a double boiler and heat until the beeswax is completely melted. Stir the mixture thoroughly to ensure it is well combined.

This is where your creativity can shine. Essential oils, vitamin E, and even honey can be added to your salve or balm to enhance its therapeutic properties and scent. Essential oils such as lavender, tea tree, or peppermint can be added for additional antimicrobial and soothing effects. Vitamin E serves as a natural preservative and skin conditioner.

1. **Adding Essentials**: Once the beeswax and oil mixture is off the heat but still liquid, add a few drops of essential oils. If using vitamin E, a small amount can be stirred in as well.

2. **Pouring the Mixture**: Quickly pour the mixture into prepared tins or jars. As the salve cools, it will solidify, so work efficiently.

Once cooled and solidified, label your containers with the ingredients and the date of creation. Stored in a cool, dark place, salves and balms can last up to a year or longer, especially if vitamin E is added as a preservative.

Using your homemade salves and balms is straightforward. Apply them liberally to the affected skin areas, and enjoy the soothing and healing effects. Whether it's a calendula salve for healing wounds or a peppermint balm for refreshing dry, tired feet, your creations can be tailored to meet specific needs or preferences, making them invaluable additions to your home health care.

The process of making salves and balms not only equips you with effective remedies for everyday ailments but also deepens your connection to herbal medicine. Each step, from selecting herbs to pouring the final product, is imbued with intention and care, reflecting the holistic ethos of natural healing.

3. Brewing Medicinal Teas and Infusions

Brewing medicinal teas and infusions is an age-old practice, a gentle yet profound way to access the healing properties of herbs. Whether you are seeking relaxation, digestive relief, or immune support, the right herbal tea can provide therapeutic benefits alongside the simple comfort of a warm, soothing drink. Understanding how to properly brew these teas and infusions ensures that you maximize the medicinal qualities of the herbs involved.

Medicinal teas and infusions differ primarily in the parts of the plant used and the steeping time involved. Teas generally use the delicate parts of the plant, such as leaves, flowers, and sometimes seeds, and require a shorter steeping time. Infusions, on the other hand, are best suited for the tougher parts like roots, barks, and berries, requiring a longer steeping process to extract the active compounds effectively.

To make a medicinal tea:

1. **Selecting Herbs**: Choose high-quality, dried herbs specific to your health needs. For calming effects, chamomile or lavender are excellent choices. For digestion, consider ginger or peppermint.

2. **Boiling Water**: Start with fresh, cold water and bring it to a boil. The temperature of the water is crucial — too hot, and you might destroy delicate compounds; too cool, and you may not extract the full benefits.

3. **Steeping**: Place about one teaspoon of dried herbs per cup of water in a tea infuser or teapot. Pour boiling water over the herbs and cover to prevent the escape of volatile oils. Steep for 5 to 10 minutes, depending on the desired strength.

4. **Straining and Serving**: Strain the herbs out and serve the tea. You may add honey, lemon, or other natural flavor enhancers to taste.

Infusions are designed to draw out the deeper, more robust compounds from hardier plant materials:

1. **Choosing Material**: Select the appropriate dried roots, barks, or berries. Dandelion root, burdock, and cinnamon are potent choices for various health benefits.

2. **Ratio and Water**: Use a larger quantity of herbs compared to making tea — generally a quarter to half a cup of dried herb per liter of water.

3. **Simmering**: Place the herbs in a pot, cover with cold water, and slowly bring to a gentle simmer. This slow process helps to extract a broader spectrum of medicinal compounds.

4. **Steeping Long-term**: After simmering, turn off the heat and cover the pot. Let it steep for 30 minutes to several hours, depending on how strong you need the infusion to be.

5. **Straining**: Strain the mixture through a fine mesh or cheesecloth. The resulting infusion can be stored in the refrigerator for a few days.

Combining different herbs in a single tea or infusion can amplify their effects. However, understanding which herbs complement each other is crucial to avoid any adverse reactions. For instance, combining ginger with peppermint can enhance digestive benefits, while echinacea paired with elderberry might offer superior immune support.

Practical Tips for Brewing

- **Freshness**: Always use the freshest herbs you can find for the best results. Dried herbs should be stored in airtight containers away from light and heat to preserve their potency.

- **Water Quality**: The quality of water used can affect the taste and effectiveness of the tea or infusion. Use filtered or spring water if possible.

- **Mindful Consumption**: Start with small quantities when trying a new herbal remedy to see how your body responds. Everyone's body chemistry is different, and what works for one person might not work for another.

Incorporating medicinal teas and infusions into your daily routine can be a delightful and beneficial practice. Whether it's starting the day with a vibrant cup of ginger tea to stimulate digestion or winding down with a soothing chamomile infusion at night, these herbal beverages can significantly enhance your health and well-being.

Brewing medicinal teas and infusions is more than just a culinary activity; it's a form of self-care that connects you to the natural world. Each cup offers a moment of pause, a chance to nurture yourself with the healing power of plants. By mastering these brewing techniques, you empower yourself with the knowledge to support your health naturally and deliciously.

4. Packaging and Labeling Herbal Preparations

In the intricate craft of herbal preparations, the artistry doesn't end with the creation of tinctures, salves, and teas. A critical, often overlooked aspect is the thoughtful packaging and meticulous labeling of these preparations. This ensures not only their longevity and efficacy but also that they are used safely and effectively.

Choosing the right packaging for herbal remedies is pivotal. This choice impacts the shelf life, potency, and safety of the product. Light, air, and moisture are the main antagonists in the preservation of herbal remedies, each capable of degrading the quality of the ingredients quickly. For tinctures, dark glass bottles are the standard. Amber or cobalt blue glass effectively blocks harmful UV rays, which can degrade the botanicals over time. These bottles come in various sizes, often equipped with dropper tops, which are ideal for administering liquid herbal preparations accurately.

Salves and balms fare best in containers that prevent contamination and are easy to use. Wide-mouth jars, preferably made of tinted glass or non-reactive metal, are excellent choices. They allow easy access to the product without the need to contaminate the contents with fingers or other objects.

For teas and dried herbs, airtight containers are essential. These can be glass jars or metal tins with tight-sealing lids that keep moisture and air out, preserving the herbs' potency and preventing mold growth.

Herbal remedies should be stored in a cool, dark place to preserve their therapeutic properties. Exposure to high temperatures can lead to the breakdown of active compounds, while light can accelerate chemical degradation. Even the best container can't protect its contents if stored above a sunny countertop or next to a heat source.

Labeling for Safety and Clarity

Labeling is not just a bureaucratic requisite; it's a crucial step in ensuring the safe and effective use of herbal remedies. Every label should provide essential information that includes:

- **The Name of the Product**: This might be as simple as "Chamomile Tincture" or as detailed as "Calming Chamomile and Lavender Tea Blend."
- **Ingredients**: List all ingredients used in the preparation, ideally in descending order of their proportion in the formulation. This is important for users with allergies or sensitivities and is required by regulatory bodies in many jurisdictions.
- **Date of Manufacture**: Knowing when a product was made is crucial for determining its freshness and shelf life.
- **Usage Instructions**: How much, how often, and the best way to use the preparation should

be clearly stated to avoid misuse or overconsumption.

- **Cautions and Storage Recommendations**: Include any necessary warnings about potential side effects or interactions with other medications. Instructions for how to store the remedy should also be provided to ensure it remains effective until the end of its shelf life.

In many regions, there are specific regulations governing the sale and distribution of homemade herbal remedies, particularly those intended for ingestion. It's essential to understand and comply with these regulations, which might involve listing your contact information, adhering to specific labeling guidelines, or even obtaining certification.

Beyond the basic and regulatory information, labels can serve an educational purpose. They can inform the user about the benefits of the herb, historical uses, and any supporting contemporary research. This not only adds value to your product but also helps to build trust and loyalty among your users.

Finally, the design of your labels and packaging plays a significant role in the user's experience. It should reflect the quality and ethos of the product inside. Simple, clear designs that resonate with the natural and wholesome nature of herbal remedies often speak louder than overly commercial or busy designs. The use of recyclable or biodegradable packaging materials can also reinforce the message of natural health and sustainability.

Packaging and labeling, when done thoughtfully, elevate the overall value of herbal preparations. They ensure that these natural remedies are not only appealing but also preserved and used in a manner that maximizes their benefits safely. In this way, the final touches of your herbal crafting process reflect the same care and dedication that began with the planting of a seed or the harvesting of an herb.

Embracing wellness and prevention through herbal medicine is not merely about treating ailments as they arise but nurturing a state of health that wards off disease before it begins. This chapter is dedicated to cultivating an everyday lifestyle that integrates the wisdom of herbal remedies and natural practices to strengthen your body's natural defenses and enhance overall well-being.

Herbal medicine offers more than quick fixes—it provides a pathway to long-term health by supporting body systems holistically. Here, you will discover how to use herbs not just for healing, but for thriving. From fortifying your immune system with echinacea to calming daily stresses with lavender, each section provides practical advice on using herbs to maintain balance and vitality.

The journey to sustained health is both an art and a science, involving a deep understanding of your body and the herbs that can nourish and protect it. As you turn these pages, envision yourself mastering the delicate balance of wellness, armed with nature's bounty, ready to lead a life where prevention is just as paramount as the cure.

1. Strengthening Immunity with Herbs

In the quest for holistic wellness, one of the most empowering steps you can take is to boost your immune system using natural herbs. This approach not only aligns with a self-sufficient lifestyle but also taps into the ancient wisdom of herbalism, which offers a bounty of plants known for their health-promoting properties. Understanding how to use these herbs effectively can help you maintain your health proactively, reducing reliance on conventional medical interventions.

Herbs work in harmony with the body's natural functions, enhancing its ability to fight off illnesses and maintaining overall vitality. Incorporating immune-boosting herbs into your daily regimen is not just about warding off the next cold or flu. It's about creating a foundation of health that supports your body's many systems year-round.

The immune system is a complex network of cells, tissues, and organs that work together to defend the body against pathogens. Herbs support this system in various ways, from stimulating immune responses to reducing inflammation. Some herbs have adaptogenic properties, helping to modulate the immune system by increasing its resistance to stress, which is a common precursor to immune dysfunction.

Numerous herbs are celebrated for their immune-boosting properties. Here are some of the most effective:

- **Echinacea**: Perhaps the most well-known immune-supporting herb, echinacea is believed to enhance the body's ability to fend off infections. It's especially beneficial when taken at the onset of a cold or flu. Echinacea works by increasing the production of white blood cells, which are crucial for fighting infections.

- **Astragalus**: Used in Traditional Chinese Medicine for thousands of years, astragalus supports the immune system by increasing the body's production of immune cells. It also acts as an adaptogen, helping to protect the body against stress.

- **Elderberry**: Rich in antioxidants and vitamins that can boost the immune system, elderberry is particularly effective in preventing and easing cold and flu symptoms. Its high vitamin C content and anti-inflammatory effects make it a powerful tool for immune support.

- **Garlic**: This common kitchen ingredient is a powerhouse for immune health. Garlic has antiviral, antibacterial, and antifungal properties, making it a versatile defender against various pathogens.

- **Ginger**: Another herb with broad benefits, ginger has anti-inflammatory properties that help to reduce inflammation, which is often a symptom of immune responses. It also helps to cleanse the lymphatic system, a critical part of the immune system.

To truly benefit from these herbs, consider incorporating them into your daily life in a way that feels natural and sustainable. Here are some practical ways to include immune-boosting herbs in your routine:

- **Herbal Teas**: Brewing a daily cup of herbal tea is perhaps the easiest way to consume immune-boosting herbs. Echinacea, elderberry, and ginger can be steeped as teas. Enjoying these beverages can be a calming ritual that also serves your immune system.
- **Tinctures and Supplements**: For a more concentrated dose, you might consider herbal tinctures or capsules. These are particularly useful for herbs like astragalus and garlic, which you might not consume in large quantities in your diet.
- **Culinary Uses**: Incorporating garlic and ginger into your cooking not only enhances flavor but also boosts your immune system. Use these herbs liberally in soups, stews, stir-fries, and other dishes.
- **Preventive Practices**: During peak cold and flu season, increase your use of these herbs as a preventive measure. Making an elderberry syrup or increasing your intake of echinacea tea can help fortify your body's defenses.

While herbs are a fantastic way to boost your immunity, they work best when paired with a healthy lifestyle. Ensuring adequate sleep, managing stress, maintaining a healthy diet, and getting regular exercise are all essential components of a robust immune system. Herbs should be part of a holistic approach to wellness that includes these other elements.

Before incorporating new herbs into your regimen, it's important to understand that some herbs can interact with medications or other supplements. Consulting with a healthcare provider, especially if you have underlying health conditions or are taking medications, is advisable. This is not only a safety consideration but also ensures that you are using herbs in a way that is most beneficial for your health.

2. Stress Management and Sleep Aids

Managing stress and promoting restful sleep are critical components of maintaining robust health and wellness. In a world where both physical and mental demands are incessant, harnessing the calming powers of nature through herbs not only soothes the immediate stresses but also equips the body to handle future challenges with resilience. Herbs that aid in stress reduction and sleep support do so by calming the mind, reducing anxiety, and fostering deeper sleep, which in turn, enhances the body's healing processes.

Chronic stress and inadequate sleep can undermine health profoundly, affecting everything from immune function to mental clarity. Prolonged stress may lead to a host of issues including hypertension, fatigue, and even depression. Similarly, poor sleep can impair the body's ability to repair itself, leading to decreased cognitive function and increased susceptibility to illness. Integrating herbal remedies can be an effective strategy to mitigate these effects by providing natural, gentle support to the nervous system.

Several herbs have been cherished through the ages for their relaxing and sedative properties. Here's a look at some of the most potent:

- **Valerian Root**: Known for its sedative qualities, valerian root can be especially helpful in easing anxiety and promoting deep, restorative sleep. It increases the levels of a neurotransmitter called gamma-aminobutyric acid (GABA) in the brain, which helps to regulate nerve cells and calm anxiety.

- **Chamomile**: With its mild sedative effects, chamomile is ideal for pre-sleep relaxation. It is also effective in managing mild stress. Chamomile tea, enjoyed before bed, can help prepare the mind and body for sleep.

- **Lavender**: Renowned for its calming aroma, lavender can reduce anxiety and improve sleep quality. It can be used in various forms such as essential oils, herbal sachets, or infused in teas.

- **Ashwagandha**: This adaptogen helps the body manage stress more effectively. It can reduce cortisol levels, enhance stamina, and support overall well-being. Ashwagandha is particularly beneficial for those who feel drained due to stress.

- **Passionflower**: Often used for its calming effects, passionflower can help alleviate anxiety and insomnia. It works by boosting GABA levels in the brain, promoting relaxation.

To make the most of these herbs, consider various ways of integrating them into your daily regimen:

- **Tea Rituals**: Crafting a nightly tea ritual with herbs like chamomile or valerian can signal to your body that it's time to wind down. This not only aids in relaxation but also establishes a routine that can improve sleep consistency.

- **Aromatic Uses**: Incorporating lavender in aromatherapy practices can help reduce stress during the day and prepare the mind for sleep at night. Whether through diffusing oils or using lavender-filled pillows, these practices can enhance the overall sleeping environment.

- **Dietary Supplements**: For herbs that are less commonly used in teas or culinary practices, such as ashwagandha and passionflower, taking them in supplement form can be an effective way to ensure you are getting a therapeutic dose.

Beyond the use of herbs, creating an environment conducive to relaxation and sleep is vital. This can include:

- **Reducing Electronic Distractions**: Limiting exposure to screens and electronic devices in the evening can help decrease sensory input, which is often stimulating.

- **Comfortable Sleep Settings**: Ensure your sleeping area is quiet, dark, and cool. Consider the use of blackout curtains and comfortable bedding to improve sleep quality.
- **Regular Schedules**: Going to bed and waking up at consistent times can reinforce your body's natural circadian rhythms, making it easier to fall asleep and wake up naturally.

Alongside herbal remedies, lifestyle choices play a crucial role in managing stress:

- **Physical Activity**: Regular exercise, particularly activities like yoga or tai chi, can reduce stress and improve sleep patterns. These activities not only exert physical energy but also promote mental calmness.
- **Mindfulness and Meditation**: Practices such as meditation, deep breathing exercises, and mindfulness can greatly enhance your ability to manage stress. They help in focusing the mind and calming the nervous system.

As with any herbal supplementation, it's important to understand that individual reactions can vary. What works for one person might not work for another, and some herbs might interact with medications or have side effects. Starting with small doses and paying attention to how your body reacts is crucial. Consulting with a healthcare provider before starting any new herbal regimen is advisable, particularly if you have underlying health conditions or are taking other medications. Incorporating these herbs into your life offers a profound way to enhance your body's natural healing abilities, manage stress, and promote quality sleep. These changes, in turn, can improve your overall resilience and quality of life, making you better equipped to handle the challenges of modern life with a sense of calm and preparedness.

3. Natural Antibiotics and Antivirals

Exploring the world of natural antibiotics and antivirals opens up a new dimension in the quest for health sovereignty and wellness. With rising concerns over antibiotic resistance and the desire for more holistic health approaches, turning to nature's pharmacy provides promising alternatives. These natural defenders can be essential allies in preventing and fighting infections by harnessing their inherent anti-microbial properties.

Natural antibiotics and antivirals differ from their synthetic counterparts primarily in their composition and approach. They often work not by outright killing pathogens but by strengthening the body's own defense mechanisms and creating an environment less favorable to pathogen growth. Additionally, these natural solutions frequently offer a broader spectrum of action, including anti-inflammatory, immune-boosting, and tissue-healing properties. Natural antibiotics have been used for centuries as effective remedies against bacterial infections.

Here are some of the most potent:

- **Garlic**: Known for its strong antimicrobial properties, garlic contains allicin, a compound that has been shown to combat bacteria, including antibiotic-resistant strains. It's effective when eaten raw, cooked, or taken as a supplement.
- **Honey**: Particularly Manuka honey, has potent antibacterial properties and is used for wound care, helping to prevent infections and promote healing.
- **Goldenseal**: Often used for its antibiotic properties, goldenseal contains berberine, a compound effective against bacteria and fungi. It is commonly used for respiratory tract infections and digestive issues.
- **Oregano Oil**: Known for its antibacterial and antiviral properties, oregano oil can be a powerful agent against sinus infections and other bacterial infections. It should be diluted before use, as it is very potent.

Antiviral herbs can reduce the severity and duration of viral infections by boosting the immune system and preventing the virus from replicating. Some noteworthy antivirals include:

- **Elderberry**: This berry is well-known for its effectiveness in treating flu symptoms and reducing the duration of the illness. It has antiviral properties against several strains of influenza.
- **Echinacea**: Popularly used for colds and flu, echinacea can help reduce the chances of catching a cold by boosting the immune system and has some direct antiviral effects.
- **Licorice Root**: Contains glycyrrhizin, which has shown effectiveness against viruses like hepatitis and HIV in clinical studies. It's also used for its soothing properties on the throat and digestive tract.

To make effective use of these natural remedies, consider the following practical applications:

- **Dietary Integration**: Incorporating garlic and honey into your daily diet not only enhances flavor but also provides ongoing antimicrobial benefits. Garlic can be added to a variety of dishes, and honey can be used as a natural sweetener in teas or desserts.
- **Supplementation**: For more concentrated doses, supplements like oregano oil capsules or echinacea extract can be taken, especially during the cold and flu season or at the first sign of an infection.
- **Topical Applications**: Honey can be applied topically to minor cuts and burns to prevent infection and promote healing. Similarly, oregano oil, when diluted with a carrier oil, can be applied to areas affected by fungal infections.

While natural antibiotics and antivirals are generally safe, they are not without risks and limitations. It's crucial to consider the following:

- **Allergies and Sensitivities**: Always test for allergies when trying a new herb, especially when applying it topically.
- **Interactions with Medications**: Some natural remedies can interact with prescription medications. For instance, licorice root can affect blood pressure and might interfere with certain heart medications.
- **Quality and Purity**: The effectiveness of herbal remedies heavily depends on their quality and purity. Source your herbs and supplements from reputable suppliers to ensure they contain potent, uncontaminated ingredients.
- **Consultation with Professionals**: Before beginning any new treatment regimen, especially if you have existing health conditions or are taking other medications, consult with a healthcare provider knowledgeable about both conventional and herbal medicine.

Embracing natural antibiotics and antivirals is about more than just treating infections. It's part of a broader commitment to living a healthier, more sustainable life. By relying on natural substances, not only can you reduce your ecological footprint, but you also empower yourself by developing knowledge and skills that enhance your self-sufficiency in healthcare.

In conclusion, whether you are looking to treat specific ailments or simply aiming to fortify your health against pathogens, natural antibiotics and antivirals can play a pivotal role in your wellness strategy. By integrating these natural defenders into your lifestyle, you embrace a form of healthcare that is not only effective but also harmonious with nature's rhythms.

4. Adapting Herbal Practices for Different Life Stages

Embracing herbal medicine involves recognizing that our needs change as we journey through different stages of life. From the boundless energy of childhood to the reflective pace of elder years, each phase brings its unique wellness challenges and opportunities. Adapting herbal practices to these stages not only maximizes their effectiveness but also ensures safety and suitability for the individual's age and health condition.

Herbal Care in Childhood

Children represent both resilience and vulnerability, requiring a gentle approach to herbal intervention. Their bodies respond quickly and dynamically to natural remedies, yet their developing systems necessitate caution. Mild and safe herbs like chamomile, lavender, and fennel are staples for treating common childhood ailments such as colic, sleep disturbances, and minor skin irritations. Dosages must be carefully adjusted for body weight, and parents should always consult with a pediatric herbalist or healthcare provider before introducing new herbal treatments.

Herbal preparations for children should ideally be in pleasant forms, such as syrups, glycerites (herbal extracts made with glycerin), or herbal lollipops, which are more acceptable to a young palate. Education about the benefits and flavors of herbs can begin early, incorporating herbal teas and infused waters into their routine, fostering a lifelong appreciation for natural health.

Teenage Years: Addressing New Challenges

As children grow into teenagers, their bodies and hormones undergo significant changes that can be supported by herbal remedies. Skin conditions like acne can be effectively managed with herbs that have cleansing and anti-inflammatory properties, such as burdock root or calendula. Emotional fluctuations that often accompany adolescence may be smoothed by adaptogens like ashwagandha or nervines such as St. John's wort.

In addition, this life stage is an ideal time to educate young individuals about the responsible use of herbs, including the importance of sourcing, ethical considerations, and the understanding of herbal actions on the body. Encouraging teenagers to participate in making their own herbal preparations, such as acne creams or stress-relieving teas, empowers them and deepens their connection to herbal medicine.

Adulthood: Maintaining Balance and Preventing Chronic Conditions

During adulthood, the focus often shifts towards maintaining health and preventing the onset of chronic conditions that commonly arise later in life. Adaptogenic herbs like Rhodiola and Holy Basil can enhance resilience to stress, a common feature of adult life. For adults dealing with the demands of work and family, herbs that support cognitive function and energy levels, such as ginkgo biloba and Siberian ginseng, can be invaluable.

Women in their reproductive years may benefit from herbs that regulate menstrual cycles and support reproductive health, such as vitex or raspberry leaf. Men might find saw palmetto and nettle root helpful for supporting prostate health as they age.

The Elder Years: Supporting Vitality and Managing Age-Related Issues

As individuals transition into their elder years, the focus of herbal practice often shifts towards managing chronic conditions and enhancing quality of life. Herbs such as hawthorn for heart health and turmeric for its anti-inflammatory properties become particularly important. Managing joint health with herbs like devil's claw or supporting memory with Ginkgo biloba can contribute significantly to maintaining independence and vitality.

Elderly individuals also need to be mindful of potential interactions between herbal remedies and pharmaceuticals, a common concern given the higher likelihood of multiple medication use in this age group. Close collaboration with healthcare providers is essential to safely integrate herbal practices with conventional medical treatments.

Integrating Herbal Practices Throughout Life

Throughout all life stages, continuity and personalization in herbal practice enhance its benefits. Keeping a health journal can be a practical way to track which herbs have been most effective at different times, providing a valuable tool for adjusting personal herbal practices as one ages. Additionally, regular consultations with herbalists and health care providers ensure that herbal remedies are used safely and effectively, tailored to the changing needs of the individual.

By thoughtfully adapting herbal practices to the specific requirements of each life stage, herbal medicine can provide a continuous thread of wellness that supports a lifetime of health.

BOOK 2: PREPPER'S NATURAL MEDICINE RECIPES

THE HERBALIST'S KITCHEN: A PREPPER'S GUIDE TO NATURAL REMEDIES

CHAPTER 1: HERBAL TINCTURES AND EXTRACTS

Diving into the world of herbal tinctures and extracts opens a doorway to the potent, concentrated essence of nature's healing powers. This ancient art, once the realm of apothecaries and healers, is now accessible to anyone seeking to bolster their health through natural means. Tinctures and extracts capture the medicinal properties of herbs in a form that is both easy to administer and long-lasting, making them ideal for anyone looking to integrate herbal remedies into their busy modern lifestyles. As we explore this chapter, you'll learn not only how to craft these potent liquids but also understand the principles that ensure their effectiveness. Whether you're soothing a troubled digestive system, boosting your immune response, or simply seeking to enhance your daily wellness routine, the versatility of tinctures and extracts makes them invaluable tools in your natural health arsenal.

By harnessing the simple yet profound techniques of herbal extraction, you are continuing a tradition that has supported human health for centuries. This chapter will guide you through selecting the right herbs, choosing your solvents, and mastering the extraction processes that maximize the potency and purity of your herbal remedies. Prepare to empower yourself with knowledge that turns everyday herbs into powerful allies for your health.

1. Simple Tincture Techniques

Creating herbal tinctures is a timeless method to extract and preserve the medicinal properties of herbs. This technique, simple and efficient, allows you to capture the essence of herbs in a concentrated form, making it easy to administer doses that support health and wellness. Tinctures are not only a staple in herbal medicine due to their long shelf life but also because they are highly portable and convenient for on-the-go use.

A tincture is typically made by soaking herbs in alcohol to extract the active compounds from the plant material. The alcohol acts as a solvent, pulling out the chemicals responsible for the herb's healing properties. This method preserves these properties for a long period, allowing you to have a readily available supply of herbal remedies at your fingertips.

To start making your own tinctures, you need only a few basic supplies:

- **Herbs**: Fresh or dried herb of your choice, depending on the remedy you wish to prepare.
- **Solvent**: High-proof alcohol (at least 40% alcohol by volume, such as vodka or brandy) is preferred because it is effective at extracting a wide range of plant compounds and preserves the tincture for years.
- **Jar with a tight-fitting lid**: This will be used to infuse the herbs in the alcohol.
- **Strainer or cheesecloth**: For separating the solid herb parts from the liquid tincture after the infusion process.

Simple Steps to Make a Tincture

1. **Choosing Your Herbs**: The first step is selecting the herbs you want to use. Whether you're looking to create a tincture for relaxation, such as lavender or chamomile, or something to bolster immune health, like echinacea or elderberry, the herb you choose will depend on the effects you desire.

2. **Preparation of Herbs**: If using fresh herbs, chop them finely to maximize the surface area that will contact the alcohol. Dried herbs can be lightly crushed or used whole. The finer the herb, the more surface area is exposed, and the more efficiently the solvent can work to pull out the desired compounds.

3. **Maceration**: Place the prepared herbs in your jar, filling it halfway or more, depending on the strength desired. Pour the alcohol over the herbs until the jar is nearly full, ensuring the herbs are completely submerged to prevent mold growth. Seal the jar tightly.

4. **Infusion Time**: Store the jar in a cool, dark place for about 4 to 6 weeks. This is the maceration period, during which the alcohol extracts the active compounds from the herbs. Shake the jar daily to help mix the contents and improve extraction.

5. **Straining**: After the infusion period, strain the liquid through a cheesecloth or fine mesh

strainer into another clean jar or bottle. Squeeze or press the herb matter to extract as much

6. liquid as possible.

7. **Bottling and Storing**: Transfer the strained tincture into dark glass bottles (preferably with dropper lids for easy use). Label the bottles with the name of the herb and the date of creation. Store the bottles in a cool, dark place; tinctures can be used effectively for up to several years.

Tips for Successful Tincture Making

- **Alcohol Choice**: While vodka is a popular choice due to its neutral flavor and 40% alcohol content, some herbs, like resins or barks, may require higher alcohol strengths (around 60-70%) to dissolve all beneficial compounds effectively.

- **Herb-to-Alcohol Ratio**: A common starting point is a 1:5 ratio of herbs to alcohol for dried herbs, or a 1:2 ratio for fresh herbs. This can be adjusted depending on the specific herb and desired strength.

- **Timing**: While 4-6 weeks is standard, some herbs may benefit from a longer or shorter maceration time based on their specific properties and the solvent strength.

To use a tincture, the general guideline is to start with 1-2 ml, which can be taken directly under the tongue or diluted in a small amount of water or tea. This method allows the active compounds to enter the bloodstream quickly. However, the dosage can vary depending on the herb and the individual's needs.

The beauty of tinctures lies not just in their effectiveness but in their simplicity and the personal connection you forge with your health practices. As you blend, infuse, and strain, you're participating in an age-old tradition of self-care, creating remedies that not only soothe and heal but also connect you to the natural world.

2. Extracts for Digestive Health

Herbal extracts have long been celebrated for their ability to soothe and support the digestive system, a critical component of overall health. The digestive tract is not only responsible for the assimilation of nutrients and elimination of waste but also plays a crucial role in immune function and even emotional well-being. Thus, maintaining digestive health is paramount, and natural extracts offer a gentle, effective way to support this complex system.

Digestive problems can range from occasional upset stomach, bloating, and gas to more chronic conditions such as irritable bowel syndrome (IBS), gastroesophageal reflux disease (GERD), and inflammatory bowel diseases (IBD) like Crohn's and ulcerative colitis. The roots of these issues can be diverse, including poor diet, stress, infections, and antibiotic use that disrupts the gut flora. Herbal extracts can help address these underlying causes and symptoms by promoting healing, reducing inflammation, and restoring balance.

Several herbs are particularly effective for digestive health, each offering unique benefits. Here are some of the most important ones:

- **Ginger**: Known for its anti-nausea effects, ginger can also promote smooth muscle relaxation in the digestive tract, which helps alleviate symptoms of gas and spasms.
- **Peppermint**: This herb is beneficial for relieving symptoms of IBS, such as bloating and intestinal spasms. The menthol in peppermint helps relax the intestinal walls, reducing cramps and spasms.
- **Fennel**: Similar to peppermint, fennel is effective in treating bloating and gas. It also supports overall digestion by promoting the function of the stomach and intestines.
- **Licorice Root**: Besides its soothing properties on the throat and stomach lining, licorice can help repair stomach mucosa and restore balance. It is particularly useful for those suffering from GERD and ulcers.
- **Chamomile**: Often used for its calming effects, chamomile also helps alleviate digestive discomfort by reducing inflammation and relaxing muscle contractions in the gastrointestinal tract.

Creating extracts for digestive support involves a few key steps that ensure you capture the most beneficial properties of the herbs.

1. **Herb Selection and Preparation**: Choose high-quality, organic herbs to avoid pesticides and other chemicals. Fresh herbs should be clean and free from mold and decay, while dried herbs should be aromatic and vibrant in color.
2. **Choosing the Solvent**: While alcohol is a common solvent in tincture making, for those sensitive to alcohol or preferring a non-alcoholic version, glycerin or vinegar can be effective alternatives. These solvents still extract a broad range of beneficial compounds but are gentler on the stomach.
3. **Extraction Process**:
   - **Alcohol Extracts**: Combine the herbs with a high-proof alcohol like vodka or brandy, generally at a ratio of 1 part herb to 5 parts alcohol. Seal in a glass jar and store in a cool, dark place, shaking daily for 4-6 weeks before straining.
   - **Glycerin Extracts**: Mix one part finely chopped or ground dried herbs with three parts glycerin and one part water. Store as you would an alcohol extract.
   - **Vinegar Extracts**: Use apple cider vinegar in place of alcohol, following the same proportions and process.

4. **Straining and Storing**: After the extraction period, strain the herbs using cheesecloth or a fine mesh strainer, squeezing or pressing the plant material to extract as much liquid as possible. Bottle the extract in clean, dark glass bottles and label with the herb, solvent, and date. Store in a cool, dark place.

To use the extracts, the dosage will depend on the strength of your tincture and the specific needs of your digestive system:

- **General Digestive Support**: 1-2 droppers full of extract can be taken in water or tea, usually before meals to aid digestion or after meals to soothe symptoms like bloating or gas.
- **Acute Symptoms**: For acute conditions like nausea or cramping, smaller doses more frequently throughout the day can be effective.

While herbal extracts are a powerful tool in managing digestive health, they should be part of a broader approach that includes dietary changes, stress management, and regular exercise. Ensuring a diet rich in fiber, fermented foods, and plenty of fluids can support the digestive system naturally. Additionally, practices like yoga and meditation can help manage stress, which is often a significant factor in digestive issues.

In integrating herbal extracts into your digestive health regimen, you're adopting a time-honored approach to wellness that supports not just the physical but also the emotional and mental aspects of health. Through these natural remedies, you can nurture your body's digestive system and enjoy greater vitality and well-being.

3. Immune-Boosting Formulas

In the heart of holistic health lies the importance of a robust immune system, a true testament to the body's innate ability to defend itself against illnesses. Herbal tinctures play a pivotal role in this arena, offering concentrated, immune-boosting remedies that enhance bodily functions and stave off pathogens. Understanding how to craft and use these tinctures can empower you to maintain your health throughout the seasons, particularly during times when your body is more susceptible to external threats.

Several herbs are known for their immune-enhancing properties. These herbs can stimulate the immune system, increase the production of immune cells, or possess antimicrobial properties that help fight off viruses and bacteria. Here's a closer look at some of the most effective immune-boosting herbs:

- **Echinacea**: Renowned for its ability to enhance the immune system, echinacea is often used at the onset of colds and flu. It works by increasing the body's production of white blood cells and can reduce the duration of illnesses.

- **Astragalus**: This herb is a staple in Traditional Chinese Medicine for its immune-boosting and antiviral properties. It is particularly noted for its ability to deepen the immune function over time, making it excellent for seasonal use.
- **Elderberry**: Loaded with antioxidants and vitamins that help fight inflammation and boost the immune system, elderberry is particularly effective against respiratory symptoms associated with colds and flu.
- **Ginger**: With its impressive anti-inflammatory and antioxidative properties, ginger helps to cleanse the lymphatic system, enhancing the body's ability to fight infection.
- **Turmeric**: Known for its high curcumin content, turmeric is a powerful anti-inflammatory that can boost immune cell activity and improve the body's immune response.

Crafting your own immune-boosting tinctures involves a few straightforward steps, starting with the selection of high-quality, organic herbs. Here's how to make an effective tincture:

1. **Herb Preparation**: Begin by finely chopping or grinding your chosen herbs to increase the surface area for the extraction. You can use a single herb or a blend depending on your needs and preferences.
2. **Choosing the Solvent**: High-proof alcohol (at least 40% alcohol by volume) is ideal for extracting water-soluble and alcohol-soluble components. For those preferring a non-alcoholic version, glycerin is an excellent alternative, although it may not extract certain compounds as effectively as alcohol.
3. **Maceration**:
   - Fill a clean glass jar about half to two-thirds with your herbs.
   - Pour the alcohol or glycerin over the herbs until the jar is nearly full, ensuring the herbs are completely submerged to prevent mold growth.
   - Seal the jar and label it with the date and contents.
4. **Infusion**: Store the jar in a cool, dark place for about 4-6 weeks, shaking it daily to help the solvent extract the active compounds from the herbs.
5. **Straining**: After the infusion period, strain the mixture through a cheesecloth or fine mesh strainer into another clean jar. Press or squeeze the herbs to extract as much liquid as possible.
6. **Storage**: Transfer the strained tincture into dark glass bottles with dropper tops for easy administration. Label the bottles with the herb names and the date of bottling. Store in a cool, dark place.

To utilize your tincture:

- **Dosage**: A common dose is 1-2 droppers full (about 1-2 ml) taken 1-3 times daily during periods when you need immune support. This can be adjusted based on personal needs and specific conditions.

- **Administration**: Tinctures can be taken directly under the tongue for fast absorption, or diluted in a little water or tea if preferred.

While tinctures are a potent way to support immune health, they should be part of an integrated approach that includes a nutritious diet, adequate sleep, regular physical activity, and stress management practices. These lifestyle factors all play a significant role in the functioning of your immune system and overall health.

Herbal tinctures provide a practical and effective way to enhance your body's natural defenses. By understanding and applying the art of tincture making, you empower yourself with a tool that supports your health in a natural, personalized manner. This method not only keeps you connected with herbal traditions but also aligns with a proactive approach to wellness, allowing you to thrive in harmony with nature's bounty.

4. Herbal Tinctures for Mental Clarity and Focus

In the bustling pace of modern life, maintaining mental clarity and focus is a significant challenge, with many turning to herbal remedies as a natural way to enhance cognitive function. This subchapter explores the creation and use of herbal tinctures that are specifically designed to improve concentration, mental alertness, and cognitive longevity. These tinctures provide a viable alternative to synthetic nootropics, offering a gentle yet effective approach to boosting brain health.

Herbal tinctures for mental clarity and focus leverage the natural properties of herbs known for their cognitive-enhancing effects. These herbs often contain compounds that support brain health, enhance blood circulation to the brain, or help modulate neurotransmitter activity. By extracting these properties into a tincture, we create a concentrated, easy-to-use remedy that can be integrated into daily routines.

Several herbs stand out for their ability to enhance mental performance:

- **Ginkgo Biloba:** Renowned for its effectiveness in increasing blood flow to the brain, Ginkgo biloba is one of the most well-studied herbs for improving cognitive function. It is particularly noted for its ability to enhance memory and reduce brain fog.
- **Rosemary:** Often coined as the herb of remembrance, rosemary contains potent antioxidants that protect brain cells from damage and improve concentration and focus.
- **Gotu Kola:** This herb is used traditionally in Ayurvedic medicine to improve mental clarity. Gotu Kola assists in reducing anxiety and improving mood, which indirectly enhances cognitive abilities.

- **Bacopa Monnieri:** Also known by its Ayurvedic name Brahmi, Bacopa is effective for improving memory formation and reducing anxiety, making it an excellent herb for students and professionals alike.
- **Lion's Mane Mushroom:** Although not a traditional herb, Lion's Mane is used in herbal medicine for its ability to stimulate the production of nerve growth factors, thus supporting brain health and cognitive function.

When making tinctures intended to enhance mental clarity and focus, precision in preparation and patience in maceration are key. Here's a general guide to creating an effective cognitive tincture:

1. **Selecting Your Herbs:** Depending on your specific needs—whether it's memory, focus, or overall mental energy—choose one or a combination of the aforementioned herbs.
2. **Preparation of Herbs:** For fresh herbs, finely chop or grind them to increase the surface area exposed to the solvent. If using dried herbs, ensure they are properly desiccated and crumbled.
3. **Maceration:** Place the herbs in a glass jar and cover them with a high-proof alcohol, such as vodka or grain alcohol, which should be at least 40% alcohol by volume. The alcohol should fully submerge the herbs, with a few inches to spare at the top for expansion.
4. **Steeping:** Seal the jar tightly and store it in a cool, dark place for at least 4 to 6 weeks. Shake the jar daily to help the solvent better extract the active compounds from the herbs.
5. **Straining:** After the steeping period, strain the tincture through a fine mesh or cheesecloth into another clean jar, squeezing out as much liquid as possible.
6. **Storage:** Transfer the strained tincture into dark dropper bottles for easy dosage. Label the bottles clearly with the herb name, date of manufacture, and any usage notes.

Incorporating these tinctures into your daily regimen can be done in several ways:

- **Morning Routine:** Adding a few drops of a Ginkgo or Bacopa tincture to your morning tea can help kickstart your day with increased alertness.
- **Study Sessions:** For students, taking Rosemary or Lion's Mane tincture before study sessions can enhance focus and aid in long-term memory retention.
- **Work Challenges:** During intensive work periods, a midday dose of a cognitive tincture can help maintain high levels of mental energy and productivity.

While herbal tinctures offer significant benefits, they should be used judiciously and with consideration of potential interactions with other medications.

Always consult with a healthcare provider, especially if you have underlying health conditions or are pregnant or breastfeeding.

By embracing the power of these cognitive tinctures, you empower yourself with a natural, effective tool to enhance mental clarity and focus, helping you navigate the complexities of modern life with renewed vigor and sharpness of mind.

Exploring the craft of making salves, balms, and ointments is like uncovering an ancient form of alchemy where each ingredient is chosen for its potential to heal and soothe. These preparations are not just remedies; they are a form of care, an expression of the desire to nurture and protect the body using the bounty of nature. Unlike liquid extracts or tinctures, these thicker, more substantive concoctions create a protective barrier on the skin, delivering therapeutic herbs directly to the areas where they are most needed.

This chapter delves into the art of blending beeswax, oils, and potent herbal extracts to form comforting salves, healing balms, and protective ointments. Each formulation is tailored to address specific skin issues, from dry, cracked hands to inflamed wounds, showcasing how these simple mixtures can provide profound relief and foster healing. As you learn to infuse oils with herbal properties and blend them into soothing concoctions, you will gain not only a practical skillset but also a deeper appreciation for the simplicity and effectiveness of traditional healing practices. Through this journey, you'll see how modern hands can weave ancient wisdom into salves that comfort and cure, bridging the gap between natural medicine and everyday wellness needs.

1. Wound Healing Salve

The art of crafting a wound healing salve is a valuable skill for anyone seeking to enhance their self-care regimen with natural, effective treatments. A good wound healing salve not only soothes pain but also promotes healing and protects against infection. Using a combination of herbs known for their healing properties, this salve can be a go-to remedy for cuts, scrapes, bruises, and other minor skin injuries.

Key herbs that are beneficial in a wound healing salve include:

- **Calendula**: Renowned for its anti-inflammatory and antimicrobial properties, calendula promotes swift healing of wounds by increasing blood flow to the affected area and promoting the production of collagen proteins.

- **Comfrey**: Known as a "knit bone," comfrey is prized for its ability to mend wounds rapidly, thanks to the compound allantoin, which accelerates cell regeneration.

- **Plantain**: Commonly found in backyards and along roadsides, plantain is a powerful anti-inflammatory and antibacterial herb, making it excellent for healing and preventing infection.

- **St. John's Wort**: Traditionally used for its anti-inflammatory and antibacterial properties, this herb is particularly good for soothing pain from nerve damage associated with wounds.

- **Tea Tree Oil**: A potent antiseptic, tea tree oil is excellent for cleaning wounds and preventing bacterial infections.

To make a salve, the process involves infusing oils with your chosen herbs and then combining the infused oil with beeswax to form a semi-solid state. Here's how you can do it step by step:

1. **Herb-Infused Oil**:
   - Start by drying your herbs to remove any moisture that might cause the oil to go rancid.
   - Once dried, chop or crush the herbs to increase their surface area.
   - Place the herbs in a jar and cover them with a carrier oil such as olive oil or coconut oil. The oil should completely submerge the herbs.
   - Seal the jar and place it in a warm, dark place for about 4-6 weeks, shaking it daily. For a quicker infusion, you can gently heat the oil and herbs in a double boiler for 2-3 hours on low heat.

2. **Straining the Oil**:
   - After the infusion period, strain the oil through a cheesecloth or fine mesh strainer into a clean jar. Press or squeeze the herbs to extract as much oil as possible.

3. **Making the Salve**:
   - Measure the infused oil and pour it into a double boiler.
   - Add beeswax to the oil. A general rule of thumb is to use about 1 ounce of beeswax per

cup of oil.

- Heat the mixture until the beeswax is completely melted, stirring occasionally.
- Once melted, you can add a few drops of tea tree oil for its antiseptic properties.
- Pour the mixture into clean tins or jars and let it cool until solid.

To use the salve, simply clean the affected area with mild soap and water, pat dry, and apply a small amount of salve. Cover with a bandage if necessary. Reapply 2-3 times a day until the wound heals. The natural ingredients not only help prevent infection but also reduce inflammation and promote tissue regeneration.

Safety and Precautions

- Always patch test the salve on a small area of skin to ensure there is no allergic reaction, particularly if you have sensitive skin or are prone to allergies.
- Do not use comfrey on deep or puncture wounds as it can cause the surface to heal faster than the deeper tissues, potentially trapping bacteria.
- Ensure all containers and utensils used in making the salve are clean and sterilized to avoid contamination.

Creating your own wound healing salve is not just a practical skill—it's an empowering act that connects you to the healing traditions of the past. This salve, made with your own hands, can provide peace of mind knowing exactly what's in it and how it's made. More importantly, it allows you to harness the natural healing power of plants in a way that promotes sustainability and self-reliance.

Through this process, you gain more than just a product; you gain knowledge and a deeper connection to the natural world, enhancing both your physical health and your environmental consciousness. By choosing to create and use natural remedies, you're participating in a sustainable practice that enriches your life and ensures you're prepared to take care of minor injuries quickly and effectively.

2. Natural Pain Relief Balm

In the journey to embrace natural wellness, finding effective ways to manage pain without relying on synthetic drugs is a crucial step. Crafting a natural pain relief balm not only offers an alternative to over-the-counter options but also connects you to a more grounded, earth-connected way of living. This homemade balm can be used to soothe muscle aches, reduce inflammation, and alleviate pain from conditions like arthritis and other chronic discomforts.

The efficacy of a pain relief balm lies in the careful selection of herbs that are known for their analgesic and anti-inflammatory properties. Here are some of the most potent herbs to consider:

- **Arnica**: Known for its remarkable ability to reduce bruising and swelling, arnica is a top choice for treating physical trauma, joint pain, and muscle soreness.
- **Cayenne**: The capsaicin in cayenne pepper works by depleting the neurotransmitter responsible for sending pain signals, effectively desensitizing the area to pain.
- **Ginger**: With its powerful anti-inflammatory properties, ginger is excellent for relieving pain, especially when related to inflammation.
- **Turmeric**: Curcumin, the active compound in turmeric, is comparable in its pain relief efficacy to certain over-the-counter drugs, making it a valuable addition to any pain relief balm.
- **Peppermint and Eucalyptus**: Both of these herbs offer cooling sensations that can soothe pain and are especially beneficial for nerve pain and muscle spasms.

Making a pain relief balm involves infusing oil with effective herbs and then thickening the infusion with beeswax to create a spreadable, soothing balm. Here's how you can create your own:

1. **Herb-Infused Oil**:
   - Start by drying your chosen herbs to remove any moisture that could cause the oil to spoil.
   - Once dried, chop or crush the herbs to increase their surface area for better infusion.
   - Place the herbs in a jar and cover them with a carrier oil such as coconut or olive oil, which are known for their own anti-inflammatory and pain-relieving properties.
   - Seal the jar and let it sit in a warm, dark place for 4-6 weeks, shaking daily. For a quicker infusion, heat the oil and herbs gently in a double boiler for a few hours.

2. **Preparing the Balm**:
   - Strain the infused oil through a cheesecloth into a clean container, squeezing the herbs to extract as much oil as possible.
   - Measure the oil and pour it into a double boiler. Add beeswax to the oil (about 1 ounce of beeswax per cup of oil) to create a firmer texture.
   - Heat until the beeswax is completely melted, mixing well.
   - As the mixture melts, consider adding essential oils like peppermint or eucalyptus for additional pain-relieving effects and a pleasant scent.
   - Once everything is thoroughly mixed and melted, pour the mixture into tins or jars and allow it to cool and set.

To use the balm, simply massage a small amount into the affected area. The massaging action helps increase blood flow, while the herbs work to decrease pain and inflammation. This balm can be particularly effective when used after a warm bath or shower when your pores are open and more receptive to herbal benefits.

Tips for Effective Use

- **Patch Test**: Always do a patch test to ensure you do not have any adverse reactions to the ingredients, especially if using stronger herbs like cayenne.
- **Layering**: For enhanced benefits, layer your use of the balm with other natural pain management strategies, such as heating pads or gentle stretching exercises.
- **Consistency**: Regular application is key, especially for chronic conditions. Apply the balm at least twice a day or as needed.

Creating your own pain relief balm not only allows you to control the ingredients and avoid unwanted chemicals but also deepens your connection to the healing practices of past generations. It's a fulfilling process that enhances your self-reliance and supports a more sustainable lifestyle. As you blend these time-honored herbs into your daily routine, you'll find not only relief from pain but also an increased sense of wellness and balance. This approach isn't just about treating symptoms but nurturing a deeper harmony with the natural world.

3. Skin Care Ointments

In the realm of natural health care, the skin is often a primary focus because it not only protects our bodies from the outside world but also serves as a reflection of internal health. Creating skin care ointments with natural ingredients can provide nourishing, healing, and protective benefits that rival, and often surpass, those found in commercial products. These ointments can soothe dry skin, heal abrasions, and even aid in reducing the appearance of scars and blemishes.

The selection of herbs and other natural ingredients in your ointment should be targeted toward specific skin needs. Some of the most effective ingredients include:

- **Calendula**: Known for its soothing properties, calendula is excellent for healing cuts, burns, and other skin irritations due to its anti-inflammatory and mild antimicrobial effects.
- **Comfrey**: Comfrey is celebrated for its ability to heal skin rapidly due to the presence of allantoin, which stimulates cell growth and repair.
- **Tea Tree Oil**: With powerful antiseptic properties, tea tree oil can help treat acne and other bacterial skin infections.
- **Lavender**: Renowned for its calming aroma, lavender also has anti-inflammatory and antibacterial properties, making it perfect for general skin care, especially for soothing and healing irritated skin.
- **Shea Butter**: A superb moisturizer, shea butter is rich in vitamins and fatty acids, which are crucial for rejuvenating and maintaining healthy skin.

Creating a homemade ointment involves a few key steps:

1. **Choosing Your Base**: The base of your ointment can greatly affect its texture and skin-feel. Common bases include shea butter, coconut oil, or even a more solid base like beeswax for a thicker ointment.

2. **Infusing Oils**: Begin by infusing your chosen base oil with herbs. This can be done by gently heating the oil with herbs such as calendula or comfrey in a double boiler for several hours until the oil has taken on the color and properties of the herbs.

3. **Melting and Mixing**: Once your oil is infused, strain the herbs and return the oil to the double boiler. Add beeswax to thicken the mixture to the desired consistency. For every cup of infused oil, adding about a quarter cup of beeswax should create a firm but spreadable ointment.

4. **Adding Essential Oils**: Once the beeswax and infused oil are thoroughly mixed and off the heat, stir in essential oils like tea tree or lavender for their therapeutic benefits. Be sure to add these last to prevent heat from diminishing their potency.

5. **Cooling and Setting**: Pour the mixture into clean, sterile jars and allow it to cool completely. As it cools, the ointment will thicken and set.

To use the ointment, apply a small amount to the affected area of the skin. For dry skin or eczema, applying the ointment to slightly damp skin can help lock in moisture. For wounds, gently spread a thin layer over the clean, dry area.

Tips for Effective Use

- **Storage**: Store your ointment in a cool, dry place. Natural ointments can melt in high heat or become too firm in cold. If your ointment melts, simply re-solidify it in a cooler environment or the refrigerator.

- **Patch Testing**: Before applying widely, especially for sensitive or damaged skin, do a patch test on a small area to ensure there is no allergic reaction.

- **Longevity**: Natural ointments do not contain preservatives, so they have a shorter shelf life than commercial products. Use clean hands or an applicator to scoop the ointment to keep it free from bacteria.

Crafting your own skin care ointments isn't just about treating skin issues; it's about taking control of what you put on your body and reducing your reliance on commercially manufactured products. This practice encourages a deeper connection to the ingredients and the natural world, and fosters a greater understanding of how various components can affect and enhance skin health.

By choosing to make your own ointments, you embrace a tradition of self-care that places wellness and sustainability at the forefront.

4. Balms for Respiratory Health

In the heart of herbal healing practices lies the art of crafting remedies that not only soothe the body but also support its natural healing processes. Among the most cherished of these are balms for respiratory health, which provide comfort and relief during times of congestion, coughs, and respiratory distress. These balms harness the potent properties of herbs known for their ability to ease breathing, clear nasal passages, and calm irritated lungs.

Key to creating effective respiratory balms is the selection of appropriate herbs. Herbs like eucalyptus, peppermint, and thyme are stalwarts in respiratory care due to their expectorant, antiseptic, and soothing properties. Eucalyptus, for instance, is renowned for its ability to clear nasal congestion and combat respiratory infections. Its high content of cineole, a potent expectorant, helps break up mucus and reduces inflammation.

Peppermint contains menthol, which provides a cooling sensation that can ease breathing and relieve throat irritation. Thyme, rich in thymol, acts as an excellent cough suppressant and has antibacterial properties that help in treating respiratory infections.

The process of making a respiratory balm involves infusing oils with selected herbs and then blending these infused oils with beeswax to create a soothing, spreadable balm. Here's a step-by-step guide to making your own:

1. **Herb Infused Oil:**
   - Start with a carrier oil such as coconut oil, olive oil, or almond oil. These oils are excellent for their skin-soothing properties and serve as a base for the herbal infusion.
   - Add dried herbs to the oil in a ratio of one part herb to ten parts oil. Gently heat the oil and herbs in a double boiler, keeping the temperature low to avoid frying the herbs. Maintain the heat for about 2 to 3 hours to allow the oil to fully absorb the active compounds of the herbs.
   - Strain the oil through a cheesecloth into a clean jar, squeezing out as much oil as possible from the herbs.

2. **Creating the Balm:**
   - Measure the infused oil and prepare beeswax in a ratio of one part beeswax to five parts oil. This ratio can be adjusted depending on the desired consistency of the balm.
   - Gently heat the beeswax and infused oil together in a double boiler until the beeswax is completely melted and mixed uniformly with the oil.
   - Once melted, remove from heat and allow it to cool slightly. At this point, essential oils such as eucalyptus or peppermint can be added for additional therapeutic benefits. Add about 10 drops of essential oil for each ounce of balm for optimal effectiveness.

3. **Setting the Balm:**
    - Pour the mixture into small tins or jars. Let the balm set at room temperature or place it in the refrigerator to speed up the solidification process.
    - Once solid, cover the containers with lids to preserve the balm's aromatic and therapeutic properties.

To use, simply rub a small amount of the balm on the chest, throat, or under the nose. The warmth of the skin helps release the vapors of the essential oils, which are then inhaled, providing immediate respiratory relief. For nighttime use, applying the balm before sleep can help manage coughs and ensure a more restful sleep.

While these balms are generally safe for most people, it is essential to perform a patch test first to ensure there is no allergic reaction to any of the ingredients. Additionally, the use of essential oils, particularly potent ones like eucalyptus and peppermint, should be moderated, especially in balms intended for use by children.

Herbal balms for respiratory health not only offer natural and effective relief but also empower individuals to take an active role in managing their health with gentle, plant-based solutions. By creating and utilizing these balms, one embraces the age-old wisdom of herbal care, tailored to meet modern needs.

Stepping into the world of medicinal teas and beverages is akin to entering a garden of healing—a place where each leaf and flower holds the potential to soothe, invigorate, and restore. This chapter is dedicated to the art and science of blending these natural elements into drinks that do more than quench thirst; they nurture the body and soul.

The tradition of brewing medicinal teas is ancient and universal, crossing cultures and generations. It is a practice that engages the senses, combines the practical with the mystical, and turns the simple act of drinking tea into a therapeutic ritual. Here, you'll learn not only the properties of various herbs but also how to combine them into concoctions that can calm a troubled mind, energize a tired body, and fortify a weakened immune system.

As we explore soothing herbal teas, energizing morning brews, and nighttime relaxation blends, you'll discover how easy and satisfying it is to incorporate these healthful beverages into your daily routine. Each sip offers a moment of peace and a step toward wellness, inviting you to slow down and savor the flavors nature provides. This isn't just about drinking tea; it's about enriching life with each cup.

1. Soothing Herbal Teas

The gentle art of preparing soothing herbal teas is much like crafting a symphony—each herb contributes its unique notes to harmonize into a blend that comforts the mind and heals the body. Herbal teas have been revered across cultures for centuries, not only for their delightful taste but also for their ability to alleviate ailments ranging from the mundane to the chronic. This section explores how you can harness these healing powers to create teas that soothe, relieve, and rejuvenate.

Each herb in a tea blend serves a purpose, bringing not just flavor but specific therapeutic benefits:

- **Chamomile**: Perhaps the quintessential soothing herb, chamomile is known for its mild sedative effects that can help reduce anxiety, soothe nerves, and promote better sleep. Its anti-inflammatory properties also make it beneficial for soothing digestive upsets.
- **Lavender**: Famous for its calming scent, lavender also extends its soothing effects when ingested as a tea. It's particularly effective in alleviating stress, reducing anxiety, and even mitigating mild pain.
- **Peppermint**: With a refreshing and invigorating flavor, peppermint tea is excellent for digestive health, helping to relieve symptoms of bloating, cramping, and nausea.
- **Lemon Balm**: Known for its ability to ease insomnia and anxiety, lemon balm can also help improve cognitive function and reduce symptoms of stress.
- **Valerian Root**: Often used in teas meant for relaxation or sleep, valerian root has potent calming effects that can help manage stress and insomnia.

The process of making herbal tea is as much about the ritual as it is about the result. Here's how you can create your own soothing teas:

1. **Selecting Your Herbs**: Choose fresh or dried herbs based on the effects you desire. For a tea that promotes relaxation and sleep, chamomile and lavender make a great pair. For digestive relief, peppermint or ginger are excellent choices.
2. **Proportions and Blending**: When blending herbs, start with equal parts of each and adjust based on your taste preferences and the desired strength of each herb's effect. Typically, use one to two teaspoons of dried herbs per cup of water, or double that if you are using fresh herbs.
3. **Brewing the Tea**:
   - Boil water and let it cool for a minute to avoid scorching the herbs, which can alter their medicinal properties.
   - Pour the hot water over the herbs in a teapot or a cup, then cover to prevent the steam and volatile oils, which contain much of the herbs' therapeutic properties, from escaping.

- Let the tea steep for about 5 to 10 minutes. The longer it steeps, the stronger the flavor and therapeutic benefits.
- Strain the herbs from the water and enjoy. You can add honey or lemon to taste, depending on your preference.

Incorporating soothing herbal teas into your daily routine can significantly enhance your quality of life by providing a natural way to reduce stress and promote relaxation. Over time, these teas can help:

- **Improve Sleep Quality**: Herbs like chamomile and valerian root are effective in promoting a restful night's sleep, helping you to wake up refreshed and revitalized.
- **Reduce Anxiety and Stress**: Regular consumption of lavender or lemon balm tea can help maintain a calm and stable mood, supporting overall mental health.
- **Enhance Digestive Health**: Teas made from peppermint or ginger support digestion and can relieve symptoms of indigestion, bloating, and gas.

Creating your own blends allows you to tailor the flavors and therapeutic effects to suit your needs. Experiment with different combinations of herbs to discover what works best for you. Here are a few tips for customization:

- **Experiment with Flavors**: Mix and match herbs not only for their health benefits but also to achieve flavors that you enjoy. Adding a bit of cinnamon or licorice root can enhance the natural sweetness of your tea without sugar.
- **Adjust Brewing Time and Temperatures**: Some herbs, like green tea leaves or more delicate flowers, may require cooler water or shorter steeping times to prevent bitterness.
- **Use High-Quality Herbs**: The quality of the herbs you use will significantly affect both the taste and the healing properties of your tea. Whenever possible, choose organic herbs to avoid pesticides and other chemicals.

Soothing herbal teas offer a simple yet profound way to engage with the healing power of plants. Whether you are winding down after a long day or seeking to soothe an upset stomach, these teas provide a delicious and therapeutic solution that honors the body's natural rhythms and needs.

2. Energizing Morning Brews

Starting your day with an energizing morning brew can transform your morning ritual into a vibrant, health-enhancing practice. Unlike the jolt from caffeine-laden coffee, herbal morning brews offer a sustained boost of energy through natural ingredients that support your body's own energy production mechanisms without the subsequent crash. These beverages are crafted from herbs that invigorate the senses, enhance mental clarity, and fortify the body for the day ahead.

Certain herbs are particularly valued for their energizing properties. These herbs not only stimulate the body and mind but also offer nutritional benefits that support overall health:

- **Green Tea**: Rich in antioxidants and a natural source of caffeine, green tea provides a gentler rise in energy compared to coffee. The presence of L-theanine also helps improve focus and mental clarity.
- **Ginseng**: Known for its revitalizing properties, ginseng boosts energy levels and can help improve cognitive function. It is also thought to help balance the release of stress hormones in the body, making it an excellent choice for a stress-filled day.
- **Guarana**: This herb contains a higher concentration of caffeine than most other plants but is absorbed more slowly, offering a longer-lasting energy boost without the crash.
- **Yerba Mate**: Popular in South America, yerba mate is another herb rich in antioxidants, vitamins, and minerals, providing both a stimulant effect and nutritional benefits.
- **Rhodiola Rosea**: Often used in traditional medicine to combat fatigue and improve energy levels, Rhodiola is known for enhancing stamina and mental capacity.

Creating an energizing morning tea or beverage involves thoughtful selection of herbs that not only stimulate energy but also taste great.

1. **Herb Selection**: Choose one or more of the energizing herbs mentioned above based on your taste preferences and desired effects. For a balanced energy boost that includes mental clarity, mixing green tea or yerba mate with ginseng or Rhodiola can be effective.
2. **Preparation**: To prepare your tea, use about one teaspoon of dried herbs per cup of boiling water. If you are using roots like ginseng, these might need to be simmered in water for a longer period to extract their active ingredients.
3. **Brewing**:
   - Boil water and let it cool slightly before pouring over the leaves to preserve the integrity of the herbs' oils and flavors.
   - Steep the tea for 5-10 minutes, depending on the herb. Leaf-based teas like green tea need less time, while denser materials like roots may benefit from longer steeping.
4. **Enhancing Flavor and Benefits**: To enhance the flavor and add to the energizing effects, consider adding natural sweeteners like honey or a slice of lemon. Fresh ginger or a dash of cinnamon can also complement the flavors while adding their own health benefits.

Integrating these energizing brews into your morning routine can help set a positive tone for the day. Here are some tips for making the most of your morning beverage:

- **Consistency**: For the best results, make your herbal brew part of your daily morning ritual. Consistent use can help sustain energy levels and improve overall vitality over time.

- **Mindful Drinking**: Take the time to enjoy your brew. Savor the aroma and the flavors, and allow yourself a moment of calm to prepare mentally and physically for the day ahead.
- **Hydration**: Remember that hydration is key to maintaining energy levels. Starting your day with a herbal brew also contributes to your daily fluid intake, supporting overall health.

In addition to providing an energy boost, these morning brews offer various health benefits. Antioxidants and vitamins found in herbs like green tea and yerba mate contribute to long-term health improvements, including enhanced immune function and reduced inflammation. Adaptogenic properties of herbs like Rhodiola and ginseng help improve your body's response to stress, making you more resilient over time.

The beauty of herbal teas lies in their versatility. You can adjust the strength of the brew, mix different herbs for varied effects, and add flavors according to your preference. This not only makes your morning routine more enjoyable but also allows you to tailor the benefits to meet your specific health needs.

Embracing the practice of starting your day with an energizing herbal beverage is a delightful and healthy tradition that offers more than just a caffeine fix. It invites you to engage with natural rhythms, supports sustained energy throughout your day, and enriches your health with every sip.

3. Nighttime Relaxation Blends

In the gentle quiet of the evening, a carefully crafted nighttime relaxation blend of herbal tea can become a cherished ritual that sets the stage for a restful night. These blends harness the natural properties of herbs to calm the mind, relax the body, and prepare you for deep, rejuvenating sleep. Such teas not only help in winding down from the day but also enhance the quality of sleep, providing a foundation for improved health and well-being.

The key to an effective nighttime tea lies in the selection of herbs that are known for their sedative, calming, and sleep-inducing properties:

- **Chamomile**: Often the star of nighttime teas, chamomile is revered for its mild sedative effects, making it a go-to herb for reducing anxiety and settling the stomach before bed.
- **Lavender**: Known for its soothing aroma, lavender also has properties that can reduce stress, alleviate headaches, and induce a state of calm relaxation.
- **Valerian Root**: This herb is one of the most potent natural sedatives, known to improve the quality of sleep and ease the time it takes to fall asleep.
- **Lemon Balm**: Coupled with its pleasant, mild lemon scent, lemon balm has been used to ease insomnia, anxiety, and stress, helping to quiet the mind and body.
- **Passionflower**: Known for its calming effects, particularly helpful in combating insomnia

and agitation, passionflower is a great addition to any relaxation tea blend.

Creating your own nighttime tea blend involves more than just mixing herbs. It's about understanding how the flavors and properties of each herb complement each other to enhance their collective effects.

1. **Proportions and Preparation**:
   - Start with a base of chamomile, known for its universally soothing effects.
   - Add smaller amounts of other herbs based on their strength. Valerian root is potent, so it should be used sparingly.
   - Consider the flavors as well as the effects—lavender and lemon balm not only add calming properties but also pleasant, soothing flavors.

2. **Brewing the Tea**:
   - Boil water and let it cool for a minute to avoid overheating the herbs, which can destroy some of their delicate flavors and properties.
   - Pour the hot water over the herbs and cover your pot or cup to keep the essential oils from evaporating.
   - Steep for 10 to 15 minutes. Longer steeping times release more of the soothing oils and flavors.

3. **Enhancing the Tea**:
   - To enhance sweetness and add another layer of flavor, consider a spoonful of honey, which also offers additional soothing properties.
   - A slice of fresh ginger or a cinnamon stick can be added during the brewing process for those who prefer a bit of spice, which also aids digestion.

Incorporating herbal teas into your nightly routine can help signal to your body that it's time to wind down. Here's how you can make the most of this ritual:

- **Consistency is Key**: Try to drink your tea around the same time each evening to help establish a routine, which can further aid in signaling to your body that it's time to prepare for sleep.
- **Create a Calm Environment**: Enjoy your tea in a quiet space where you can relax without distractions. This might be a cozy corner of your living room or in your bedroom, perhaps while reading or listening to soft music.
- **Mindful Consumption**: Savor each sip, focusing on the warmth and flavors. Mindfulness can enhance the relaxation effects of your tea by keeping you present and engaged in the ritual.

The benefits of nighttime teas extend beyond just helping you sleep. Regular consumption can lead to:

- **Improved Sleep Quality**: Ingredients like valerian root and chamomile help increase the quality of your sleep, not just the quantity.
- **Reduced Evening Anxiety and Stress**: Herbs like lemon balm and passionflower have anxiolytic properties that help lower stress and anxiety levels, which can improve overall relaxation.
- **Holistic Well-being**: Engaging in a nightly ritual of tea drinking can improve your overall sense of well-being and can be a comforting, nurturing practice in self-care.

Feel free to experiment with different combinations of herbs to find what works best for you. Each person's body reacts differently to herbs, and what is soothing for one might be less effective for another. Trial and error with different herbs and proportions can lead you to your perfect bedtime blend.

Embracing the practice of drinking a soothing herbal tea at night is not just about seeking better sleep—it's about creating a moment of tranquility in your day. This simple practice can be a profound act of self-care that nurtures not just the body but also the soul.

4. Herbal Teas for Digestive Health

Embracing the nurturing power of nature, herbal teas have long been celebrated for their ability to heal and soothe. Among their many benefits, their role in promoting digestive health stands out as particularly significant. Digestive discomforts such as bloating, indigestion, and irregularity can disrupt daily life, but the gentle support of herbal teas can provide substantial relief and foster long-term digestive wellness.

The choice of herbs for teas aimed at digestive support is guided by their medicinal properties that target various aspects of the digestive process. Herbs that stimulate digestion, alleviate gas, soothe cramps, and encourage regular bowel movements are particularly valuable. Each herb has a unique profile of benefits, making it suitable for different digestive needs:

- **Peppermint**: One of the most beloved digestive herbs, peppermint tea is excellent for relieving gas and bloating. Its antispasmodic properties help relax the muscles of the digestive tract, easing cramps and spasms that can cause discomfort.
- **Ginger**: Known for its warming properties, ginger tea is ideal for stimulating digestion and improving circulation. It is particularly effective in treating nausea and is a trusted remedy for morning sickness and motion sickness.
- **Chamomile**: Renowned for its calming effects, chamomile is equally beneficial for soothing

the digestive system. It can help reduce inflammation, alleviate cramping and treat an upset stomach.

- **Fennel**: With a flavor reminiscent of licorice, fennel tea is excellent for combating flatulence and improving overall digestion. Fennel seeds can be brewed into a tea that also supports the liver and can help reduce feelings of fullness after a heavy meal.

- **Licorice Root**: Though it should be used with caution due to its potent properties, licorice root tea can soothe the stomach lining, ease reflux, and balance the digestive environment.

Creating an effective digestive tea involves more than simply steeping a single herb. Blending several herbs can enhance the therapeutic effects, as the combined properties work synergistically to address multiple symptoms simultaneously. Here is how you can craft a balanced digestive tea blend:

1. **Select Your Base Herb**: Choose an herb that addresses the primary symptom you wish to alleviate. For general digestive discomfort, peppermint or chamomile makes an excellent base.

2. **Add Supporting Herbs**: Incorporate herbs that complement the action of your base herb. For example, adding ginger to peppermint can enhance its digestive stimulating properties, while fennel can amplify the anti-gas benefits.

3. **Consider Flavor and Potency**: Balancing flavors is crucial, as the taste can affect the tea's enjoyability and thus its usage. Also, consider the potency of herbs like licorice, which should be used in moderation.

4. **Steeping the Perfect Cup**: To extract the full medicinal qualities, steep your tea blend in hot water for 5 to 10 minutes. Covering the teapot or cup while steeping helps trap the essential oils and flavors within the tea, enhancing both its efficacy and aroma.

For those suffering from chronic digestive issues, incorporating herbal teas into daily routines can provide ongoing support. Here are a few tips:

- **Morning**: Start the day with a cup of ginger tea to stimulate digestive juices and prepare the stomach for the day's meals.

- **Post-Meal**: Sipping on a cup of peppermint or fennel tea after meals can ease digestion and prevent discomfort.

- **Evening**: A cup of chamomile tea in the evening can help relax the digestive system and prepare the body for restful sleep.

While herbal teas are generally safe, they can interact with medications and affect underlying health conditions. Always consult with a healthcare provider, especially if you have chronic digestive issues or are on medication.

Herbal teas for digestive health offer a gentle, natural way to enhance digestive wellness.

By understanding the properties of various herbs and how they can be blended, anyone can craft a personal tea remedy that not only alleviates discomfort but also actively supports digestive health, contributing to overall well-being and vitality.

In the tapestry of natural medicine, syrups, elixirs, and tonics are the threads that intertwine efficacy with pleasure, delivering potent herbal benefits in forms that are both delightful and palatable. This chapter delves into the art and science of concocting these liquid remedies, each designed to address specific health needs—from soothing a sore throat with a rich, herbal syrup to boosting overall vitality with an invigorating elixir.

The tradition of crafting these remedies is rooted in ancient practices where the wisdom of herbs was distilled into liquid forms that could be easily consumed and rapidly absorbed by the body. Whether it's a syrup that coats and calms, an elixir that invigorates the spirit, or a tonic that detoxifies and balances, these preparations combine the best of flavor and function.

Here, you'll learn how to harness these traditional methods to create remedies that not only foster health but also please the senses and nourish the soul. Through step-by-step guides, you'll explore how simple ingredients from nature can be transformed into healing, energizing, and revitalizing beverages that support daily wellness and contribute to a sustainable lifestyle.

1. Cough Syrups and Sore Throat Remedies

Harnessing the power of nature to soothe a sore throat or calm a persistent cough is an ancient practice that modern herbalists continue to refine. Herbal cough syrups and sore throat remedies embody the convergence of traditional wisdom and contemporary needs, offering effective and natural alternatives to over-the-counter medications. These remedies not only ease discomfort but also work with the body's natural defenses to promote healing.

The effectiveness of any herbal remedy hinges on understanding the properties of its components. Herbs such as marshmallow root, licorice root, and slippery elm have mucilaginous properties that soothe irritated mucous membranes. Honey, often used as a base in syrups, is prized for its antibacterial and soothing qualities. Thyme and ginger bring antispasmodic benefits, reducing the cough reflex and calming the throat.

A well-crafted herbal cough syrup can offer relief from both dry and productive coughs while providing nourishment and boosting the body's immune response.

Ingredients:

- **Honey**: A natural cough suppressant and wound healer, honey is an excellent base for any syrup.
- **Marshmallow Root**: Soothes irritation and inflammation in the throat and contains mucilage that coats the throat.
- **Licorice Root**: Acts as a demulcent (soothing agent) and expectorant, helping to ease coughing and bronchial issues.
- **Thyme**: With strong antimicrobial properties, thyme is excellent for respiratory infections and coughs.
- **Ginger**: A potent anti-inflammatory that can help with pain and nausea associated with severe coughs.

Preparation:

1. **Herb Decoction**:
   - Begin by making a strong decoction. Combine 1 part dried marshmallow root, 1 part licorice root, 1/2 part thyme, and a few slices of fresh ginger with 4 parts water.
   - Simmer this mixture until the volume is reduced by half to concentrate the decoction.
2. **Straining and Sweetening**:
   - Strain the herbs, pressing to extract as much liquid as possible.
   - While the decoction is still warm, add an equal part of honey, stirring until fully dissolved. The warmth will also activate the honey's natural preservative qualities, extending the shelf life of your syrup.

3. **Bottling**:
   - Pour the finished syrup into sterilized glass bottles.
   - Store in the refrigerator where it will keep for up to 2-3 months.

For direct sore throat relief, a soothing gargle can be made from herbs that reduce pain, kill bacteria, and calm inflammation.

Ingredients:

- **Salt**: Natural antiseptic properties help reduce swelling and clear infections.
- **Sage**: Anti-inflammatory and antibacterial, sage is a traditional remedy for sore throats.
- **Apple Cider Vinegar**: Helps break up mucus and is naturally antibacterial.

Preparation:

1. **Herbal Infusion**:
   - Steep 1 part dried sage in 2 parts boiling water for 10-15 minutes.
   - Mix in a teaspoon of salt and a tablespoon of apple cider vinegar.
2. **Use**:
   - Gargle the mixture several times a day, especially after eating or before bed, to relieve pain and prevent bacterial growth.

Incorporating these remedies into daily life during the cold and flu season can provide ongoing support and prevention. Regular use of syrups can not only soothe symptoms but also fortify the body's defenses during vulnerable times.

Tips for Effective Treatment

- **Consistency**: For best results, especially when battling an active cough or sore throat, remedies should be used consistently several times a day.
- **Hydration**: Keeping well-hydrated is essential when dealing with respiratory infections, as it helps to thin mucus and keep mucous membranes moist.
- **Warmth**: Keeping the throat warm with a scarf can help ease the irritation that comes with a persistent cough.

Creating your own cough syrups and sore throat remedies allows you to adjust flavors, tailor the ingredients to your specific needs, and avoid the synthetic additives found in many commercial products. More importantly, it empowers you to take an active role in your health care, using the gifts of nature to heal and comfort. This practice not only enriches your life with self-sufficiency but deepens your connection to the healing traditions that have supported human health for centuries.

2. Herbal Elixirs for Vitality

In the world of natural wellness, herbal elixirs stand out as vibrant potions crafted to enhance vitality and invigorate the spirit. These potent blends combine the raw power of herbs with the art of alchemy, creating beverages that do more than nourish—they energize and revitalize. In crafting elixirs for vitality, we draw from a rich palette of herbs known for their life-enhancing properties, creating a synergy that uplifts the body and mind.

To craft an elixir that truly enhances vitality, it's essential to choose herbs known for their energizing and restorative properties. Here are some cornerstone herbs that are renowned for boosting energy and improving overall health:

- **Ginseng**: Celebrated for its ability to enhance energy and reduce fatigue. Ginseng is a tonic herb that can support adrenal function and help the body cope with stress.
- **Ashwagandha**: Known as an adaptogen, it helps to stabilize the body's response to stress and enhances energy by improving endurance.
- **Rhodiola Rosea**: Another powerful adaptogen, Rhodiola increases energy, stamina, strength, and mental capacity.
- **Green Tea**: Contains a mild amount of caffeine and is rich in antioxidants that protect the body from oxidative stress while providing a gentle energy boost.
- **Maca Root**: Often taken as a powder, Maca supports energy metabolism and helps increase stamina and endurance.

The process of making an herbal elixir involves extracting the active components of herbs and combining them with other ingredients that enhance their effects. Here's how you can create your own vitality-boosting elixir:

Preparation:

1. **Herb Selection and Extraction**:
    - Begin by selecting your herbs. You can use these herbs in their dried form or as tinctures for ease and efficiency.
    - If using dried herbs, simmer them gently in water to create a strong decoction. For every tablespoon of mixed herbs, use about two cups of water, simmering down to one cup.

2. **Enhancing the Elixir**:
    - To the herb-infused decoction or directly to tinctures, add natural sweeteners if desired, such as honey or maple syrup, which provide flavor and additional health benefits.
    - Enhance flavor and potency with natural extracts like vanilla or citrus zest, which also offer antioxidants and other health-promoting compounds.
    - Consider adding a splash of apple cider vinegar or lemon juice for their detoxifying

properties and to add a refreshing zing.

3. **Combining Ingredients**:
    - Combine all the ingredients in a glass jar and shake well to mix. If you've made a decoction, ensure it's cooled before adding anything that may be temperature sensitive, like honey or tinctures.

To incorporate elixirs into your daily routine, consider the following tips:

- **Timing**: Consume small amounts of your elixir in the morning or early afternoon to boost your energy levels during the day without affecting your nighttime sleep.
- **Moderation**: Elixirs are potent, so a small amount goes a long way. Typically, one to two tablespoons per day are sufficient.
- **Integration**: You can drink the elixir as is, add it to a morning smoothie, or even mix it into a glass of sparkling water for a refreshing beverage.

Herbal elixirs crafted for vitality offer benefits that extend beyond mere energy enhancement:

- **Stress Reduction**: Adaptogens like ashwagandha and Rhodiola help the body adapt to stress, reducing the toll that stress can take on physical and mental health.
- **Immune Support**: Many vitality herbs also boost the immune system, helping to defend the body against pathogens.
- **Longevity and Wellness**: Regular consumption of vitality elixirs can contribute to long-term health improvements, including better cardiovascular health and enhanced metabolic function.

The beauty of homemade elixirs lies in your ability to tailor them to your specific health needs and flavor preferences. Experiment with different combinations of herbs and additives to find what works best for you and what you enjoy drinking. Over time, you can adjust the ingredients based on the seasons, your health status, and your body's needs.

Embracing the art of elixir making not only enriches your body with vital energy but also deepens your connection to the natural world. These elixirs become more than just drinks—they are a daily ritual of health and a celebration of life's vitality.

3. Detoxifying Herbal Tonics

In the pursuit of wellness, detoxification is a theme that resonates deeply within the natural health community. Detoxifying herbal tonics are beverages crafted with herbs known to cleanse and rejuvenate the body's vital systems. Such tonics enhance liver function, promote kidney health, and support the body's natural detoxification pathways. This approach to health considers the body as a whole, recognizing that to heal one part, one must consider the health of the entire system.

Detoxification is not merely about eliminating toxins—it's about strengthening the body's own cleansing systems. The liver, kidneys, and even the skin are involved in everyday detoxification. Effective herbal tonics for detoxification support these organs and their functions, enhancing the body's ability to cleanse itself naturally.

Certain herbs are celebrated for their detoxifying properties. Incorporating these into your daily regimen can significantly enhance the body's detox pathways:

- **Milk Thistle**: Known for its protective and regenerative effects on the liver, milk thistle supports liver function and helps repair liver cells.
- **Dandelion Root**: Often used for its diuretic properties, dandelion supports liver detoxification and kidney function.
- **Burdock Root**: This herb is a powerhouse for blood purification and helps to eliminate toxins through the skin and urine.
- **Nettle**: Rich in nutrients, nettle supports the kidneys in flushing out toxins and provides anti-inflammatory benefits.
- **Turmeric**: With its powerful anti-inflammatory and antioxidant properties, turmeric boosts liver function and fights oxidative stress.

Creating a detoxifying tonic involves more than just mixing ingredients; it requires an understanding of how different herbs work synergistically to support detoxification.

Preparation:

1. **Herbal Decoctions**:
   - Start by making a decoction with burdock root and dandelion root, as these tougher roots require prolonged boiling to extract their beneficial compounds. Simmer them in water for about 20-30 minutes.

2. **Infusions**:
   - Add delicate herbs like nettle and milk thistle seeds to the hot decoction after removing it from heat. These require a gentler approach, steeping in the hot liquid to draw out their nutrients without destroying heat-sensitive compounds.

3. **Incorporating Spices**:
   - Turmeric can be added during the last few minutes of simmering the decoction. Fresh turmeric root or powder works well, enhancing the tonic with its strong detoxifying and anti-inflammatory properties.

4. **Flavor and Nutrients**:
   - Enhance your tonic with lemon juice for its vitamin C and its ability to increase nutrient

absorption. A hint of raw honey can be added for flavor and additional antibacterial properties, but this is optional.

Integrating a herbal tonic into your daily routine can maximize its detoxifying effects:

- **Consistency**: For effective detoxification, consistency is key. Aim to consume your tonic 1-2 times a day, especially in the morning to stimulate the body's natural detox processes.
- **Mindful Consumption**: Drink the tonic slowly and with intention. Consider this as a time to nurture your body and honor its needs.
- **Dietary Support**: Complement your tonic with a diet rich in whole foods, minimal in processed foods, and abundant in water, fruits, and vegetables to support overall detoxification.

Detoxifying herbal tonics provide a range of benefits beyond cleansing:

- **Immune System Support**: By removing toxins and enhancing nutrient absorption, these tonics help strengthen the immune system.
- **Increased Energy and Clarity**: Clearing toxins from the body can lead to increased energy levels and mental clarity.
- **Skin Health**: As the skin is a major detox organ, supporting internal detox naturally leads to clearer, more vibrant skin.

Every individual's body is unique, and so are their detox needs. Feel free to experiment with the ratios of herbs or to introduce other detoxifying herbs that you might prefer. Adjusting the ingredients to fit your specific health circumstances or the seasons can make the tonic not only more effective but also more enjoyable to consume.

Detoxifying with herbal tonics is a gentle yet powerful way to support the body's natural functions. It's an approach that honors the body's complexity and seeks to restore balance and health in a holistic, nurturing manner.

4. Adaptogenic Tonics for Stress Relief and Energy

In an age where stress is as prevalent as the air we breathe, finding natural and effective methods to manage stress and enhance energy is crucial. Adaptogenic tonics, derived from herbs that help increase the body's resistance to physical, chemical, and biological stressors, offer a profound solution. These botanicals not only support the body's ability to cope with stress but also help to improve mental clarity, physical endurance, and emotional resilience.

Adaptogens are a unique class of herbal ingredients known for their abilities to enhance the body's resilience. They adjust their function according to the specific needs of the body, promoting homeostasis. Some of the most powerful adaptogens include Ashwagandha, Rhodiola Rosea,

Ginseng, and Holy Basil. Each of these herbs brings its own unique benefits and can be used singularly or in combination to craft tonics that support well-being.

Ashwagandha for Nervous System Support

Ashwagandha is renowned for its ability to reduce cortisol levels and combat the effects of stress. This herb enhances endurance and is incredibly beneficial for those dealing with chronic stress, anxiety, or sleep problems. Incorporating Ashwagandha into a tonic can help stabilize the mood, improve sleep quality, and boost overall vitality.

Rhodiola Rosea for Enhanced Mental Clarity and Energy

Rhodiola is particularly favored for its effects on enhancing cognitive function and physical strength. It helps in fighting fatigue and is often used by athletes to improve performance. Rhodiola works by increasing the sensitivity of neurons to dopamine and serotonin, two neurotransmitters involved in focus, memory, pleasure, and mood regulation.

Ginseng as an Energy Booster

Ginseng is one of the most popular adaptogens known for its energy-boosting properties. It increases energy production in cells, helping to combat fatigue and enhance physical activity. Ginseng is also beneficial for immune support and maintaining metabolic health.

Holy Basil for Stress Relief and Immune Health

Often referred to as Tulsi, Holy Basil helps counter metabolic stress through normalization of blood glucose, blood pressure, and lipid levels. It is also effective in elevating mood and enhancing stamina by modulating the body's stress response systems.

Crafting Adaptogenic Tonics

Creating an adaptogenic tonic involves a thoughtful blending of these herbs to target specific health concerns. Here's a basic guideline on how to create an effective adaptogenic tonic:

1. **Select Your Adaptogens**: Choose one or a combination of adaptogens based on your specific health needs—stress relief, energy boost, enhanced focus, or immune support.

2. **Decoction Base**: Start with a decoction of your chosen herbs. Simmer the herbs gently in water over a low heat for 30-60 minutes until the liquid is reduced by half.

3. **Add Natural Sweeteners**: To enhance the flavor and add nutritional value, incorporate natural sweeteners such as raw honey, maple syrup, or molasses after the decoction has cooled down slightly. These sweeteners also act as natural preservatives.

4. **Include Supporting Ingredients**: Adding other ingredients such as lemon juice for its vitamin C, ginger for its digestive properties, or cinnamon for blood sugar regulation can enhance the health benefits and flavor of your tonic.

5. **Bottle and Store**: Pour the completed tonic into clean, sterilized bottles. Store in the

refrigerator to maintain freshness. Typically, a well-prepared tonic can last up to two weeks when refrigerated.

To fully benefit from adaptogenic tonics, incorporate them into your daily routine. A morning tonic can invigorate and prepare you for the day ahead, while a mid-afternoon sip can prevent energy slumps. For stress relief and relaxation, a small dose before bedtime can promote a restful night's sleep.

Adaptogenic tonics are not just beverages; they are powerful herbal preparations that support the body's natural ability to balance stress and enhance overall health. With regular use, these tonics can improve quality of life, boost energy levels, and support mental and physical health. As with any herbal remedy, consistency and moderation are key to achieving the best results.

In the realm of natural wellness, the convenience and precision of capsules, powders, and pills allow us to harness the potent benefits of herbs in a form that fits seamlessly into our daily routines. These preparations represent a bridge between the ancient art of herbalism and the bustling rhythm of modern life, providing a practical method to incorporate natural health solutions without the time-consuming processes typically associated with traditional herbal medicine. Imagine starting your day not with a generic multivitamin, but with a capsule filled with a tailored blend of adaptogenic herbs designed to boost your resilience to stress and fatigue. Or picture soothing your digestion with a fine powder of ginger and licorice, effortlessly stirred into your evening tea. These compact forms of herbal remedies are not just about ease; they are about empowering individuals to manage and maintain their health with pinpoint accuracy.

Crafting these preparations requires a deep understanding of herbal properties and the science of extraction. It transforms raw, earthy botanicals into concentrated forms where a single capsule or a teaspoon of powder packs a therapeutic punch equivalent to several cups of brewed herbal tea. This chapter delves into the alchemy of turning loose herbs into refined powders, robust capsules, and potent pills—each a tiny but mighty ambassador of natural healing, ready to support your health journey with every swallow.

1. Preparing Herbal Capsules

Preparing herbal capsules is both an art and a science, a process where the raw power of nature is encapsulated in small, consumable forms. Herbal capsules offer the distinct advantage of delivering precise doses of herbal extracts, and they are favored for their convenience and discreetness. Whether you're at home or on the go, these little powerhouses ensure that your daily herbal regimen remains uninterrupted.

The allure of creating your own herbal capsules lies in the ability to tailor remedies specifically to your personal health needs or those of your family. This customization extends beyond mere convenience; it empowers you with control over the ingredients, ensuring that only the purest, most effective herbs cater to your wellness.

The journey of making herbal capsules begins with selecting the right herbs. The choice of herbs is guided by their intended purpose—be it enhancing sleep, boosting immune function, or calming an upset digestive tract. For instance, valerian root might be chosen for sleep, echinacea for immune support, and peppermint for digestive health.

The first step in capsule preparation is to source high-quality, dried herbs. Fresh herbs are not suitable for capsules due to their moisture content, which can lead to mold growth within the capsule. It's crucial to select organically grown herbs free from pesticides and other contaminants, ensuring that what you consume is as beneficial as nature intended.

Once you have your dried herbs, they must be ground into a fine powder. This increases the surface area, allowing for better extraction of the herbs' active components during digestion. A high-quality grinder can be used to achieve a fine consistency. Some herbs, due to their woody texture, might require a commercial mill grinder to break them down effectively.

To start, you'll need a few key pieces of equipment:

- **Herb Grinder:** To pulverize dried herbs into a fine powder.
- **Capsule Filling Machine:** This device holds the capsule halves and allows for easy filling.
- **Empty Capsules:** These are usually made from gelatin or a vegetarian substitute. They come in various sizes, with "00" being the most common for herbal use, as it holds about 735 milligrams of herb powder.

Once your herbs are powdered, the next step is blending. If you are using multiple herbs in your capsules, you need to mix them thoroughly to ensure each capsule contains a uniform dose of each herb. This blend provides a tailored solution to your health needs, harnessing the synergistic effects of multiple botanicals working in concert.

Filling capsules can be a meditative, yet meticulous process. Here's a simplified breakdown:

1. **Separate the Capsules:** Empty capsules consist of two parts; a longer body and a shorter

cap. Carefully separate these parts.

2. **Filling the Capsule Bodies:** Using a capsule machine, fill the longer part (the body) of the capsules with your herbal powder. Most capsule machines come with a tamper to help compact the powder and maximize the amount each capsule can hold.

3. **Closing the Capsules:** Once filled, the shorter part (the cap) is then placed back on the body, sealing the herbal goodness inside.

For those who fill capsules regularly, investing in a good quality capsule-filling machine can dramatically streamline the process, allowing you to prepare multiple capsules simultaneously and with consistent dosing.

Properly storing your herbal capsules is critical to preserving their potency. The capsules should be kept in a cool, dry place out of direct sunlight to prevent degradation of the herbs. An airtight container or a dark glass bottle can be ideal for keeping the capsules protected from moisture and light.

Practical Tips and Considerations

- **Labeling:** Always label your containers with the herb or blend name, the date of capsule making, and the expiration date (typically one year from making). Accurate labeling is essential for tracking your inventory and ensuring you use the oldest stock first.

- **Dosage:** Determining the correct dosage is vital. Research your herbs to understand the recommended amounts and consider consulting with a healthcare provider, especially if you are taking other medications or have underlying health conditions.

- **Testing for Allergies:** If you're trying a new herb, it's wise to test for potential allergies. Begin by taking a smaller dose of the capsule and monitor for any adverse reactions over a few days.

Creating your herbal capsules not only puts you in touch with the therapeutic virtues of plants but also deepens your connection to the Earth's natural resources. This process, rooted in ancient traditions, is enhanced by modern precision and personal care, making it a deeply rewarding component of any natural wellness journey. Through this practice, you cultivate not just health but also a profound respect for the natural world and its capacity to heal.

2. Energy and Focus Powders

In the bustling rhythm of contemporary life, maintaining energy and focus can sometimes be a Herculean task. Amidst the whirlwind of daily responsibilities, natural energy and focus powders emerge as a beacon of support, providing the nutritional backbone we need to thrive without resorting to artificial stimulants that often come with undesirable side effects. These powders harness the inherent power of nature's finest adaptogens, nootropics, and tonic herbs, offering a sustained release of energy and a sharpening of mental faculties in a way that aligns with our body's natural rhythms.

The magic of energy and focus powders lies in their composition—carefully selected herbs and plants known for their revitalizing properties. Ingredients like green tea, ginseng, and rhodiola not only enhance stamina and concentration but also improve overall vitality, making you feel more alert and engaged throughout your day.

The choice of ingredients is critical. Each herb and plant brings its unique profile of benefits, so selecting the right ones depends on understanding what each component offers:

- **Green Tea Extract:** Rich in antioxidants and a natural source of caffeine, green tea promotes sharp mental focus and provides a gentle energy boost without the jitters associated with coffee.
- **Ginseng:** Known for its ability to fight fatigue and enhance brain function, ginseng is a cornerstone of energy formulations.
- **Rhodiola Rosea:** This adaptogen is celebrated for increasing energy, stamina, strength, and mental capacity. It helps the body adapt to and resist physical, chemical, and environmental stress.
- **Bacopa Monnieri:** Often used in nootropic stacks, Bacopa improves memory formation and stress adaptation, enhancing cognitive processes involved in learning and attention.

Once you've selected your ingredients, the next step is to create a balanced blend. This involves grinding each component into a fine powder and meticulously mixing them to ensure uniformity. A coffee grinder can be used for small batches, or a high-powered blender for larger quantities. The goal is to achieve a homogenous mixture where each dose contains a balanced amount of every herb.

Integrating these powders into your daily routine can be as simple as adding a teaspoon to your morning smoothie or mixing it into a glass of water or juice. The key is consistency; natural herbs work best when used regularly over time. As for dosage, it is important to start with smaller amounts to assess your body's response, gradually increasing to the recommended dose as indicated by the herb's properties and your personal tolerance.

Practical Tips for Making and Using Energy Powders

- **Taste Management:** Natural powders can have strong, sometimes bitter flavors. Combining them with natural sweeteners like honey or blending them into fruit smoothies can make them more palatable.

- **Storage:** To preserve their potency, store your powders in airtight containers away from direct sunlight and heat. A cool, dry pantry or cupboard is ideal.
- **Labeling:** Always label your powder containers with the date of production and the expected shelf life, which typically ranges from six months to a year depending on the ingredients used.

One of the joys of making your own energy and focus powders is the ability to tailor the blend to your specific needs. If you find that certain ingredients resonate more with your body's needs, you can adjust their proportions to enhance those effects. Conversely, if something doesn't sit well with you, it can be reduced or omitted in your next batch.

While natural, these powders are potent. It's important to consider any pre-existing health conditions or medications you might be taking, as some herbs can interact with medications. Consulting with a healthcare provider, particularly one knowledgeable about herbal medicine, is a prudent step if you are unsure about the suitability of certain herbs for your health situation.

Embracing natural energy and focus powders not only elevates your daily productivity and mental clarity but also aligns with a broader commitment to health and sustainability. By choosing natural over synthetic, you support sustainable farming practices and reduce your ecological footprint, all while nurturing your body with the cleanest and most wholesome ingredients available.

In conclusion, energy and focus powders are not just supplements; they are a testament to the power of natural medicine. They represent a holistic approach to health that respects the complexities of the human body and the intricate ways in which nature supports us. Through the simple act of incorporating these powders into your daily regime, you are taking a step towards a more vibrant, focused, and energetic life, grounded in the wisdom of herbal traditions and the strength of modern botanical science.

3. Digestive Aid Pills

In our quest for holistic health, the digestive system plays a central role, acting as the foundation upon which our overall well-being is built. The creation of digestive aid pills from natural herbs provides a convenient and effective way to support this crucial system, fostering not only better digestive health but also enhancing nutrient absorption and overall vitality.

A well-functioning digestive system is essential for the proper assimilation of nutrients, the elimination of waste, and the optimal functioning of our immune system. However, modern lifestyles can often disrupt digestive harmony, leading to a range of issues from bloating and gas to more severe conditions such as irritable bowel syndrome (IBS) or inflammatory bowel diseases (IBD). Natural digestive aid pills offer a gentle yet potent way to support the digestive process and maintain this delicate balance.

The first step in creating effective digestive aid pills is selecting the right herbs that have been traditionally recognized for their benefits to the digestive system:

- **Ginger:** Renowned for its ability to ease nausea and promote gastric motility, ginger is a powerhouse when it comes to settling the stomach and enhancing digestive speed.
- **Peppermint:** With antispasmodic properties, peppermint soothes the muscles of the digestive tract, helping to relieve symptoms of IBS and other functional gastrointestinal disorders.
- **Fennel:** Used extensively in traditional medicine, fennel seeds are great for alleviating gas and bloating, making them a staple in digestive health formulations.
- **Licorice Root:** Beyond its sweet flavor, licorice root can help repair stomach lining and restore balance, particularly useful for those suffering from acid reflux and gastritis.

Once the appropriate herbs are selected, they need to be processed into a form that can be effectively used in pill making. This involves drying, grinding, and sometimes combining them with other synergistic ingredients to enhance their efficacy.

The herbs must be dried thoroughly to prevent any moisture from causing spoilage. They are then ground into a fine powder, which is the basis for the pill. This powder can be enhanced with other digestive-friendly ingredients like prebiotic fibers or other herbal extracts to boost digestive health.

The powdered herbs are mixed thoroughly to ensure a consistent blend in each pill. The mixture is then encapsulated using a pill-making machine, which can be a manual or semi-automatic device depending on the scale of production. The key is to ensure that each pill contains a uniform amount of the herbal blend, providing a standardized dose that is easy to consume.

It is important to determine the correct dosage for the herbal pills, which can vary based on the strength of the herbs used and the intended user. Generally, these pills are taken before meals to prep the digestive system or after meals to aid in digestion.

Practical Tips for Making and Using Digestive Aid Pills

- **Taste and Flavor:** Some digestive herbs can have strong or unpleasant flavors, which is a significant advantage of using pills—they can mask these tastes and make consumption more pleasant.
- **Storage:** To preserve their potency, the pills should be stored in a cool, dry place out of direct sunlight. Proper storage also ensures that the pills remain effective until their expiration date.
- **Labeling:** Accurate labeling on packaging is crucial, including the name of the product, the dosage, the manufacturing date, and the batch number. This not only helps in maintaining proper usage guidelines but also in tracking production quality.

For those seeking to enhance their digestive health naturally, incorporating these pills into daily routines can be a simple and effective addition. Whether it's taking a pill with meals to aid digestion or as part of a broader approach to health and wellness, these natural remedies can provide significant benefits without the side effects often associated with synthetic medications. Creating and using digestive aid pills is more than just about alleviating digestive discomfort—it's about empowering oneself to maintain optimal health through natural means. This approach not only supports personal health but also connects individuals to the traditional uses of plants and herbs, continuing a legacy of natural healing and respect for the body's natural processes. Through the careful selection of herbs, meticulous preparation, and thoughtful integration into daily routines, these pills offer a profound way to nurture the body from the inside out, promoting a healthy, vibrant life.

4. Herbal Formulations for Immune Support

In the pursuit of maintaining robust health, particularly in the context of an increasingly challenging environment, fortifying the immune system naturally is a priority for many. Herbal formulations—when encapsulated, powdered, or pressed into pills—provide an accessible, effective way to incorporate immune-boosting herbs into daily routines. These formulations harness the concentrated power of nature's pharmacy to support the body's defense mechanisms against pathogens.

The first step in creating effective immune support formulations is selecting the right herbs. Each herb contributes unique properties that can help stimulate and support different aspects of the immune system:

- **Echinacea**: Known for its ability to enhance the immune system by increasing the production of white blood cells, Echinacea is a go-to for both the prevention and management of colds.
- **Astragalus**: This adaptogen is revered for its deep immune-modulating effects, helping to protect the body against physical, mental, or emotional stress.
- **Elderberry**: Rich in antioxidants and vitamins, elderberry is effective in reducing inflammation and combating viral infections.
- **Garlic**: With powerful antiviral and antibacterial properties, garlic stimulates the immune system and is effective against a broad range of microbes.
- **Ginger**: Its anti-inflammatory and antioxidative properties help to prevent cellular damage and maintain immune health.

Herbal capsules provide a convenient way to consume herbs. They are particularly suitable for bitter herbs or those that require precise dosage:

1. **Powdering Herbs**: Start by finely grinding the selected herbs into a powder. A high-quality grinder can achieve a fine consistency that is crucial for effective capsule filling.

2. **Mixing Herbal Blends**: Depending on the target benefit, herbal powders can be blended to enhance their efficacy. For example, combining echinacea with elderberry can create a powerful antiviral and immune-boosting supplement.

3. **Capsule Filling**: Using a capsule machine, fill the capsules with the herbal blend. This machine ensures that each capsule is packed to a consistent density, which is essential for dosage accuracy.

Powders offer versatility and are ideal for those who prefer to integrate supplements into their food or drink:

1. **Blending Powders**: Similar to capsules, start by grinding the herbs into a fine powder. Then, mix them thoroughly to ensure a uniform blend.

2. **Enhancing Absorption**: Add natural carriers that enhance the bioavailability of the herbs, such as piperine extract, which is known to enhance the absorption of certain nutrients and compounds.

3. **Storage**: Store the powder in airtight containers away from light and moisture to preserve its potency. Powders can be added to smoothies, teas, or even sprinkled on foods.

Pills are traditionally used for their ease of use and long shelf life. They can be made by compressing herbal powders into a solid form:

1. **Binding Agents**: Natural binders such as honey, gum Arabic, or plant-based methylcellulose can be used to adhere the powders together without compromising the herbal integrity.

2. **Pressing Pills**: Using a pill press, compact the mixed and bound herbal powder into pills.

3. **Coating for Preservation**: Optionally, coat the pills with a natural agent to extend their shelf life and improve ingestion ease.

Consistency is key when using herbal formulations for immune support. Integrating these supplements into daily routines before the onset of illness can help enhance their effectiveness. Whether choosing capsules for their convenience, powders for their versatility, or pills for their portability, the consistent, mindful consumption of these immune-boosting supplements can significantly strengthen the body's natural defenses.

While herbal supplements are generally safe, they are potent and can interact with medications or affect underlying health conditions. It is crucial to consult with a healthcare provider before starting any new supplement regimen, especially for those with pre-existing health conditions or who are pregnant or breastfeeding.

In crafting these formulations, the synergy of traditional herbal knowledge with modern convenience provides a powerful tool in the quest for health and wellness. By harnessing the immune-supporting properties of herbs and delivering them in user-friendly formats, individuals can proactively contribute to their health, effectively bridging ancient herbal traditions with contemporary health needs.

BOOK 3: ADVANCED NATURAL MEDICINE FOR PREPPERS

BEYOND SURVIVAL: MASTERING ADVANCED HERBAL MEDICINE TECHNIQUES

CHAPTER 1: ADVANCED HERBAL MEDICINE MAKING

Embarking on the journey of advanced herbal medicine making is like stepping into a deeper current in the river of natural healing—a place where the elements of art and science converge with tradition and innovation. This chapter is crafted for those who have already dipped their toes into the soothing waters of herbal remedies and are now ready to wade into more intricate techniques that require a finer touch and a keener eye.

As we delve into complex formulations and precise extraction methods, we move beyond the basics, exploring the subtleties of synergy between different herbs and the meticulous conditions under which they reveal their fullest potential. Here, you will learn not just to make remedies, but to master them, understanding the why behind the what which empowers you to adapt and innovate.

This chapter promises to enhance your herbal practice, whether you aim to nurture your family's health more effectively or to share your burgeoning expertise with a wider community. It's about honing a craft that links generations and cultures—a testament to the enduring power and relevance of plant-based medicine in our lives today. With each page, you are invited to weave your own thread into the rich tapestry of herbalism, crafting remedies that resonate with the rhythms of nature and the unique needs of those they will serve.

1. Complex Formulations and Ratios

As we delve into the world of advanced herbal medicine, the ability to create complex formulations and understand the precise ratios of ingredients becomes paramount. This nuanced skill set enables the herbalist to tailor remedies specifically suited to individual needs, enhancing both the efficacy and the safety of herbal treatments.

Complex herbal formulations are more than just mixing multiple herbs together; they require an understanding of the unique properties each herb brings to the table and how these properties interact with one another. The ratios in which herbs are combined can drastically alter the effects of the final product. For example, while one herb might be used to boost the immune system, another could be added to moderate the immune response and prevent overstimulation.

Creating an effective herbal blend is akin to orchestrating a symphony. Each herb must play its part perfectly, complementing the others and working in harmony to achieve a desired therapeutic effect. This synergy not only enhances the primary benefits of the formulation but can also help mitigate any potential side effects.

Consider a common pairing: turmeric and black pepper. Turmeric contains curcumin, a compound with potent anti-inflammatory properties, but it is poorly absorbed on its own. When combined with black pepper, which contains piperine, the bioavailability of curcumin increases significantly. This kind of strategic pairing is crucial in advanced herbal medicine making.

To master complex formulations, one must first understand the actions of individual herbs. Herbs can be categorized based on their effects on the body, such as anti-inflammatory, diuretic, or nervine. Knowing these categories helps in predicting how herbs might interact when mixed.

- **Adaptogens:** Help the body resist physical, chemical, and biological stressors
- **Carminatives:** Relieve flatulence and soothe the digestive system
- **Nervines:** Support the nervous system, easing symptoms of stress and anxiety

Each category of herb plays a specific role in a formulation. By understanding these roles, an herbalist can predict and manipulate the effects of the herbal blend to better address the health conditions being targeted.

The ratios of herbs in a blend are crucial for ensuring that each herb's effects are felt without overpowering the others. There are no one-size-fits-all ratios, as the ideal balance depends on the strength of the herbs used and the desired strength of the final product.

A common method for beginners is to start with equal parts of each herb and adjust based on trial and effectiveness. However, in advanced practice, herbalists often use precise ratios based on the potency of each herb. For instance, a highly potent herb might be used in a much smaller ratio compared to a milder herb.

Creating complex herbal formulations involves trial, error, and adjustment. Here are some practical steps and considerations:

- **Start Small:** Begin with small batches of the formulation to test the synergy and effectiveness before making larger quantities.
- **Documentation:** Keep detailed records of the formulations, including the source of herbs, ratios used, methods of extraction, and any feedback received from those who use the remedy.
- **Feedback:** Feedback is crucial. Pay attention to how individuals react to the formulation and be prepared to make adjustments.

As you deepen your practice, it becomes increasingly important to consider the ethical implications of your work. Sourcing herbs sustainably, respecting traditional knowledge, and considering the ecological impact of your practice are all crucial elements of being a responsible herbalist.

- **Sustainable Sourcing:** Choose suppliers who practice ethical harvesting and farming methods.
- **Respecting Tradition:** Many herbs and formulations are rooted in indigenous and local traditions. It is important to acknowledge and respect these origins.
- **Ecological Impact:** Consider the ecological footprint of your practice, from the packaging you use to the disposal of waste materials.

Complex formulations and precise ratios are the cornerstones of advanced herbal medicine making. They require a deep understanding of plant properties, a thoughtful approach to combining ingredients, and a commitment to continuous learning and adaptation. By mastering these elements, you can craft herbal remedies that are not only effective but also tailored to the nuanced needs of those you serve. This journey, while complex, is incredibly rewarding, offering the opportunity to connect deeply with the healing power of nature.

2. Long-Term Storage Solutions

As the craft of herbal medicine making advances, one of the critical skills to hone is the ability to extend the shelf life of your preparations. Long-term storage solutions are not merely about prolonging the life of herbal remedies but are fundamental to maintaining their potency, efficacy, and safety. Understanding and implementing effective storage techniques ensures that the healing virtues of herbs are preserved from the moment they are processed until they are ready for use, regardless of the time that elapses in between.

At the heart of long-term herbal storage is an understanding of what causes herbal preparations to degrade. Factors such as light, heat, humidity, and air exposure can rapidly diminish the quality of herbal products. Each element that a remedy is exposed to can potentially start a chain reaction that leads to deterioration and loss of medicinal properties.

Light and UV Exposure

Light, particularly ultraviolet light, can break down the chemical compounds in herbs that are responsible for their therapeutic effects. UV rays can alter essential oils and other sensitive components within herbal preparations, leading to decreased effectiveness and sometimes an unpleasant alteration in flavor or scent.

Heat and Its Impacts

Heat accelerates many chemical reactions and can lead to the degradation of vital compounds in herbs. It can also promote the growth of mold and bacteria, especially in preparations that contain any trace of moisture.

Moisture and Herbal Integrity

Moisture is perhaps the greatest enemy of most dry herbal preparations. Even small amounts of humidity can encourage the growth of mold and bacteria, particularly in powdered forms or any preparation where raw plant material is exposed to air.

Oxygen and Oxidation

Exposure to air can lead to oxidation, a process that can degrade the active compounds in herbs. Oxidation affects not only the potency of an herbal remedy but can also alter its color and aroma, often signaling a reduction in its therapeutic value.

Effective Strategies for Long-Term Storage

To combat these issues, several strategies can be employed to extend the shelf life and maintain the quality of herbal medicines.

Airtight Containers

Using airtight containers is perhaps the simplest and most effective way to protect herbal remedies from air and humidity. Glass jars with tight-sealing lids are ideal as they do not interact chemically with the contents and provide a solid barrier against external conditions. Containers made of tinted glass offer the added benefit of filtering out harmful UV rays.

Cool, Dark Storage Areas

Storing herbal remedies in a cool, dark place helps mitigate the risks posed by light and heat. A cabinet in a room that does not experience dramatic temperature changes is ideal. For extra protection against heat, some practitioners use refrigeration, particularly for oil-based preparations and tinctures, which are prone to rancidity.

Desiccants for Moisture Control

Including a desiccant in storage containers, especially those containing powders or dried herbs, can absorb any moisture that might have been sealed in or that accumulates over time. Silica gel packets are a common choice, as they are effective and do not react chemically with stored herbs.

Vacuum Sealing

For products that will not be used frequently, vacuum sealing can dramatically extend shelf life by removing air from the storage environment. This method is particularly effective for bulk herbs and powders that are susceptible to oxidation.

Regular Monitoring and Rotation

Even with all precautions taken, regular monitoring of stored herbs is essential to catch any signs of degradation early. Checking for changes in color, smell, or texture can help in identifying problems before they compromise the entire preparation. Additionally, rotating stock and using older items first ensures that nothing is stored for too long.

Advanced Techniques for Sensitive Compounds

For highly sensitive compounds, more sophisticated methods like nitrogen packing, which displaces oxygen in the container, or cold storage in dark, temperature-controlled environments can be necessary. These methods are more commonly used by professional herbalists who need to ensure the viability of large quantities of herbs or particularly delicate preparations.

Effective long-term storage of herbal medicines is not just about keeping these preparations for extended periods; it is about maintaining their life force—their vital therapeutic essence—that can heal and nourish. As advanced practitioners, our approach to storing herbs should reflect our deep respect for the power of these natural remedies and our commitment to providing the highest quality care through our herbal practice. By implementing robust storage solutions, we honor the trust placed in us by those who seek our help and ensure that our herbal remedies can continue to provide comfort and healing, just as nature intended.

3. Tailoring Remedies to Individual Needs

One of the hallmarks of truly advanced herbal medicine making is the capacity to tailor remedies specifically to meet individual health needs. This personalization goes beyond basic herbal knowledge; it requires an intricate understanding of how different bodies react to herbs, as well as the nuanced interplay between various herbal constituents. It's about transitioning from creating generic herbal formulations to crafting bespoke remedies that resonate deeply with the specific conditions, constitutions, and life circumstances of those seeking healing.

Each person's body responds to herbs in a unique way, influenced by their physical constitution, lifestyle, and even emotional health. These factors determine not just which herbs should be used, but how they should be prepared and administered. For example, while chamomile might generally be soothing, its form—whether as a tea, tincture, or capsule—can greatly affect its efficacy and appropriateness for an individual.

Tailoring herbal remedies starts with a comprehensive assessment of the individual's health. This involves not only understanding the current symptoms but also gathering detailed information about their medical history, diet, lifestyle, and even emotional state. Such an assessment can uncover underlying imbalances that might influence the choice and formulation of herbs.

Herbs have different actions—some may be cooling while others are warming, some moistening while others drying. An advanced practitioner will choose herbs that balance the individual's inherent tendencies. For example, a person with a warm, dry constitution might benefit from cooling and moistening herbs like marshmallow root or licorice, rather than warming and drying herbs like ginger.

Once a thorough assessment is complete, the next step is to select and combine herbs that not only address the symptoms but also harmonize with the individual's overall constitution and health goals.

Creating a personalized herbal remedy often involves using multiple herbs that enhance or modulate each other's effects. The proportions in which these herbs are combined can significantly affect the remedy's overall impact. For instance, in a blend designed for stress relief, a base of calming herbs like lavender or valerian may be enhanced with smaller amounts of supportive herbs like ashwagandha, which acts as a tonic to the adrenal system.

The form in which an herb is given can influence its effectiveness. Some individuals may prefer teas for their gentle effect and ritualistic aspect, while others may need the convenience and concentrated potency of tinctures or pills. Tailoring the form to fit the lifestyle, preferences, and absorption ability of the individual is as crucial as selecting the right herb.

Tailoring remedies is not a one-time process. It requires ongoing evaluation and adjustment to respond to changes in the individual's condition and life circumstances.

Encouraging feedback from those using the herbal remedies provides invaluable insights into how well the formulations are working and whether they need modification. This might mean adjusting dosages, changing some of the herbs used, or even altering the method of administration depending on the feedback received.

As individuals go through life, their bodies and health needs evolve. What works at one point might become less effective as circumstances change. Regular check-ins and reassessments are essential to ensure that the herbal remedies continue to provide optimal support.

Tailoring remedies to individual needs also raises important ethical considerations. The practitioner must always respect the autonomy and wishes of the individual, providing clear information about any proposed herbal treatment and obtaining informed consent before proceeding.

Sensitive personal health information should be handled with the utmost confidentiality and respect. This builds trust and ensures that individuals feel safe sharing the details necessary to effectively tailor herbal remedies.

Advanced herbal medicine making transcends the mere mixing of herbs. It is an art that requires empathy, precision, and a deep commitment to the well-being of others. By tailoring remedies to the unique needs of each individual, practitioners provide more than just health benefits; they offer a personalized approach that acknowledges the whole person—body, mind, and spirit. This personalized approach not only enhances the effectiveness of the treatments but also deepens the therapeutic relationship, fostering a greater sense of health and harmony.

4. Enhancing Bioavailability of Herbal Remedies

In the intricate world of herbal medicine, the effectiveness of a remedy is not solely determined by the herbs selected but also by how well these herbs are absorbed into the body—a concept known as bioavailability. Enhancing the bioavailability of herbal remedies ensures that the active compounds are more readily absorbed by the body, thereby increasing the efficacy of the herbal preparation.

Bioavailability refers to the proportion of an ingredient that enters the circulation when introduced into the body and so is able to have an active effect. Factors that influence herbal bioavailability include the physical and chemical properties of the herb, the form of the herbal remedy, and how it is administered.

Methods to Enhance Bioavailability

1. **Optimizing Extraction Methods**: The process by which the medicinal compounds are extracted from the herb can greatly influence bioavailability. For instance, tinctures that use alcohol as a solvent often extract a wider range of water-soluble and fat-soluble compounds than water extracts, such as teas. Ultrasonic and heat-assisted extractions can also increase the efficiency of the extraction process and thus the bioavailability of the compounds.

2. **Using Bioenhancers**: Bioenhancers are substances that enhance the bioavailability and efficacy of a drug or herbal remedy without any therapeutic activity of their own when used alone. One of the most commonly used natural bioenhancers is piperine, a compound found in black pepper, which has been shown to enhance the absorption of various nutrients such as turmeric, ashwagandha, and green tea. Incorporating small amounts of piperine with these herbs can significantly increase their effectiveness.

3. **Nanotechnology**: Applying nanotechnology in herbal medicine involves designing nano-sized particles of the active ingredients which can be absorbed more easily by the body. This not only enhances the absorption rate but also improves the distribution of the compounds within the body, potentially increasing the herb's efficacy.

4. **Liposomal Formulations**: Liposomes are tiny spheres made of cholesterol and naturally occurring phospholipids, which can encapsulate herbal extracts. These spheres protect the active compounds from degradation during digestion and enhance their absorption through the intestinal wall.

5. **Formulating with Fats**: Many herbal compounds are fat-soluble, meaning they dissolve better in fats. By combining these herbs with oils or fats in a formulation, their absorption can be significantly improved. For example, the curcumin in turmeric is better absorbed when taken with fats like coconut oil or olive oil.

Practical Applications

To apply these methods, herbal medicine practitioners can start by selecting the appropriate method based on the specific herb and desired outcome:

- **Tinctures and Extracts**: Opt for alcohol-based tinctures when working with herbs that contain both water-soluble and fat-soluble compounds. Consider heat or ultrasonic-assisted extraction methods to maximize the yield and potency.

- **Tablets and Capsules**: For herbs taken in tablet or capsule form, consider using piperine as a bioenhancer or formulating with liposomal technology to improve delivery and absorption.

- **Topical Applications**: When preparing salves and creams, incorporating liposomal formulations can enhance the delivery of the active compounds through the skin.

While enhancing bioavailability is beneficial, it is important to consider the increased potency of the herbal remedy and its potential interactions with other medications. As always, it is crucial to consult with healthcare professionals when integrating these advanced practices, particularly when treating specific health conditions or when other medications are involved.

Enhancing the bioavailability of herbal remedies represents a significant advancement in herbal medicine, allowing practitioners to achieve greater therapeutic effects with smaller quantities of herbs. By employing sophisticated extraction techniques, utilizing bioenhancers, and embracing innovative technologies such as nanotechnology and liposomal delivery, herbalists can significantly increase the impact and efficiency of their remedies, making herbal medicine an even more powerful tool in the pursuit of health and wellness.

Navigating the challenges of chronic conditions with herbal medicine offers a beacon of hope for those seeking alternatives to conventional treatments. Chronic illnesses, often lifelong companions, affect every facet of life, demanding solutions that not only alleviate symptoms but also enhance overall well-being. This chapter delves into the role of herbal medicine as a profound ally in the management of chronic conditions such as arthritis, diabetes, and heart disease, among others.

Here, we explore how natural remedies can be integrated thoughtfully and effectively into long-term health strategies. By harnessing the nuanced power of herbs, we can address not just the physical symptoms of chronic conditions but also the emotional and psychological aspects that accompany long-term illness. This holistic approach emphasizes not only relief but also resilience and vitality, offering a pathway to improved health that aligns with the body's natural rhythms and healing capacity. Through a blend of scientific research and time-honored herbal traditions, this section provides insights into creating personalized herbal protocols that support the body's own healing mechanisms. This approach not only seeks to mitigate the symptoms commonly associated with chronic diseases but also to restore a harmonious balance within the body, thus enhancing the quality of life for those affected.

1. Managing Chronic Pain Naturally

Chronic pain, a pervasive issue that affects millions, often becomes a daunting adversary in the lives of those it touches. Conventional medicine, while effective in many cases, offers solutions like opioids that can have undesirable side effects and risk dependency. It's here, in the gentle embrace of the earth's flora, that we find alternative, sustainable approaches for managing chronic pain naturally through herbal medicine.

The philosophy of herbal pain management is rooted in restoring balance and reducing inflammation, rather than merely masking symptoms. Herbs offer complex chemical frameworks that can support the body's own healing mechanisms, providing relief that aligns with our natural processes.

Pain, especially chronic, often stems from inflammation or nerve disturbance. To treat it effectively with herbs, it's crucial to understand its origin—be it arthritic inflammation, neuropathic pain, or muscle tension. Each type of pain calls for a different herbal strategy, making a tailored approach necessary.

Several herbs have been recognized for their efficacy in reducing pain and inflammation:

- **Turmeric:** Known for its active compound curcumin, turmeric is highly regarded for its anti-inflammatory properties. It works by inhibiting key enzymes in the inflammation pathway, making it comparable to certain over-the-counter anti-inflammatory drugs.

- **Willow Bark:** Often referred to as nature's aspirin, willow bark contains salicin, a precursor to salicylic acid (the active ingredient in aspirin). It's especially effective in treating pain associated with inflammation, such as back pain and osteoarthritis.

- **Ginger:** Besides its well-known gastrointestinal benefits, ginger is an excellent anti-inflammatory that can help alleviate muscle and joint pain. Its compounds block inflammation pathways in a similar manner to turmeric.

- **Devil's Claw:** A lesser-known but potent anti-inflammatory herb, devil's claw has been shown to relieve pain and improve mobility in conditions like arthritis.

- **Capsaicin:** Derived from chili peppers, capsaicin is used topically to desensitize pain receptors on the skin, providing relief from nerve, muscle, and joint pain.

Developing an effective herbal pain management plan involves considering the type of pain, its severity, and the individual's overall health and preferences. This may include using herbal teas, tinctures, capsules, or topical preparations like salves and creams.

- **Teas and Decoctions:** For systemic inflammation, a daily regimen of herbal teas made from ginger or turmeric can help reduce overall pain levels.

- **Tinctures and Capsules:** More concentrated forms like tinctures or capsules might be suitable for more severe or persistent pain conditions, providing a more potent dose that can be easily regulated.
- **Topical Applications:** Salves containing capsaicin or essential oils from eucalyptus and peppermint can be applied directly to the affected areas, offering localized relief without systemic side effects.

Herbal remedies require monitoring and adjustments, much like any therapeutic approach. Keeping a pain diary can be an effective way for individuals to track their pain levels and the effects of the herbs, providing valuable feedback that can be used to adjust dosages or formulations.

While herbs are natural, they are not free from causing side effects or interactions with other medications. It's crucial for anyone considering herbal remedies for pain to consult with a healthcare provider, particularly if they are already taking pain medication. Ensuring compatibility and safety is paramount in any complementary therapy plan.

Part of using herbal medicine effectively is understanding not just what herbs to use but how they interact with the body and other treatments. Empowering those suffering from chronic pain with knowledge about their conditions and herbal options available can help them make informed decisions about their health management strategies.

Herbal medicine provides a viable, gentle alternative for managing chronic pain, aligned with the body's natural healing processes. By personalizing herbal treatments and combining them with knowledge and appropriate safety measures, individuals can find significant relief from chronic pain, enhancing their quality of life without the heavy reliance on pharmaceutical options. This approach is not just about alleviating symptoms but fostering a deeper harmony within the body, promoting long-term health and well-being.

2. Herbal Approaches to Mental Health

The mind, a complex and delicate tapestry of neural pathways, emotions, and biochemical reactions, often mirrors the health of the body. When mental health falters, the repercussions ripple across all aspects of life, suggesting a need for supportive care that includes, but also transcends, conventional treatments. Herbal approaches to mental health offer a holistic avenue for restoration, working subtly and deeply to rebalance the body's own healing capabilities.

Herbal remedies provide a gentler alternative to pharmaceuticals, often with fewer side effects, making them an appealing option for long-term management of mental health. These remedies, rooted in ancient traditions, offer support for conditions ranging from anxiety and depression to stress and insomnia.

Herbs act on the body and mind through several mechanisms: some may directly affect the brain's chemical neurotransmitters, while others work by moderating the body's stress response systems. For example, adaptogens help the body cope with stress, potentially reducing the psychological impact of stressors, while nervines directly calm the nervous system.

Several herbs are particularly noted for their beneficial effects on mental health:

- **St. John's Wort:** Widely recognized for its effectiveness in treating mild to moderate depression, St. John's Wort works by influencing neurotransmitters that affect mood and emotions.
- **Ashwagandha:** An adaptogen that helps to stabilize mood and combat stress, ashwagandha supports overall emotional balance.
- **Valerian Root:** Known for its sedative qualities, valerian is often used to alleviate anxiety and improve sleep quality, which in turn supports mental health.
- **Lavender:** Not just a pleasant aroma, lavender has potent anxiolytic effects that can calm anxiety without sedation.
- **Passionflower:** Often used for its calming effects, passionflower can be particularly effective for managing anxiety and insomnia, helping to restore a more peaceful mental state.

Integrating Herbal Remedies Into Mental Health Regimens

Incorporating herbal remedies into a mental health care plan involves more than just choosing the right herb. It's about understanding how to use these herbs effectively to maximize their therapeutic benefits while minimizing potential side effects.

Teas and Tinctures

Herbal teas and tinctures offer an accessible way to consume mental health-supportive herbs. The ritual of preparing and sipping tea can itself be calming, while tinctures provide a more concentrated dose that can be easily controlled and adjusted.

Capsules and Tablets

For those who prefer convenience or dislike the taste of herbs, capsules and tablets can be an effective alternative. These forms ensure consistent dosages and can make integrating herbs into daily routines seamless.

Topical Applications

Essential oils derived from herbs like lavender can be used topically or diffused into the air to provide calming benefits. Aromatherapy can be particularly effective for immediate stress relief and is easily incorporated into daily routines.

Monitoring and Adjustments

Herbal treatments for mental health conditions need to be monitored closely. What works for one person might not work for another, and the effectiveness of herbs can change over time.

- **Regular Check-Ins:** Regular consultations with a healthcare provider can help assess the effectiveness of the regimen and make necessary adjustments.
- **Holistic Approach:** Herbs are best used as part of a broader approach to mental health that includes dietary changes, regular physical activity, and psychotherapy when necessary.

Safety and Interactions

While herbs are natural, they are not without risks. Many can interact with conventional medications, particularly psychiatric drugs, and can have potent effects that need to be managed under the guidance of a healthcare professional.

- **Consultation:** Always consult with a healthcare provider, particularly one knowledgeable in both herbal and conventional psychiatric treatment, before starting any new herbal regimen, especially for serious mental health conditions.

Embracing herbs for mental health reflects a commitment to managing well-being in a holistic, integrated manner. This approach not only addresses the symptoms of mental health issues but also supports the body's overall resilience, promoting a deeper, sustained return to wellness. As with all aspects of health, the most effective care is personalized, carefully considered, and continuously adapted to meet the changing needs of the individual. Through the thoughtful integration of herbal medicine, individuals can reclaim a sense of balance and peace in their mental landscape.

3. Herbs for Heart Health and Diabetes

In the quest for holistic health, the heart and metabolic processes take center stage, especially considering the modern epidemic of heart disease and diabetes. Herbal remedies offer a comforting bridge between traditional health practices and contemporary medical insights, providing a natural means to support heart health and manage diabetes. By integrating specific herbs into daily routines, individuals can nurture their cardiovascular system and help regulate blood sugar levels, promoting overall well-being and longevity.

Herbal Allies for Heart Health

The heart, a symbol of life and vitality, requires nurturance and protection. Herbs that support cardiovascular health typically work by improving blood flow, reducing arterial inflammation, and stabilizing blood pressure.

Hawthorn: The Heart Tonic

Hawthorn is perhaps the most celebrated herb for heart health, esteemed for its rich bioflavonoid content that helps enhance heart function and increase blood flow to the heart muscle itself. It gently dilates blood vessels, easing the workload on the heart while it fortifies the integrity of vascular walls.

Garlic: Natural Blood Thinner

Garlic is renowned not only for its unmistakable aroma but also for its ability to improve heart health. It helps lower blood pressure, reduce cholesterol, and act as a natural blood thinner, making it a powerhouse for preventing atherosclerosis and heart disease.

Arjuna: Ayurvedic Heart Healer

Used for centuries in Ayurvedic medicine, Arjuna bark is effective in treating heart disease due to its cardioprotective and cardio-strengthening abilities. It helps in managing heart rhythm and is particularly beneficial for those recovering from cardiac events.

Herbs for Managing Diabetes

Managing blood sugar levels is crucial for those battling diabetes. Several herbs have shown promise in not only helping to manage glucose levels but also in addressing the secondary issues associated with diabetes, such as oxidative stress and fat metabolism.

Cinnamon: Blood Sugar Regulator

Cinnamon is more than just a kitchen spice; it has the remarkable ability to help regulate blood sugar levels and improve insulin sensitivity. Regular consumption can be a helpful addition to a diabetic diet, aiding in the metabolic processing of sugars and fats in the diet.

Fenugreek: Glycemic Control

Fenugreek seeds are high in soluble fiber, which helps slow down carbohydrate digestion and absorption, thus preventing sugar spikes after meals. Its amino acid content also stimulates insulin production, enhancing glycemic control.

Bitter Melon: Natural Insulin

Bitter melon closely resembles cucumber but with a rough, bumpy skin. It contains at least three active substances with anti-diabetic properties, including charantin, which has been found to have a blood glucose-lowering effect, and an insulin-like compound known as polypeptide-p.

Crafting a Herbal Regimen for Heart and Diabetic Health

Integrating these herbs into daily life requires thoughtful consideration of individual health profiles and current medications. Here are some ways to incorporate these herbs effectively:

Teas and Infusions

Herbal teas are an excellent way to consume heart and diabetes-friendly herbs daily. Hawthorn and cinnamon can be brewed to create soothing teas that not only offer medicinal benefits but also provide hydration.

Capsules and Tinctures

For those who prefer a more concentrated form or do not enjoy the taste of certain herbs, capsules and tinctures offer an alternative. These forms allow for precise dosing and can be easier to incorporate into a daily routine, especially for managing diabetes.

Dietary Integration

Incorporating garlic and cinnamon into the diet is another effective strategy. These herbs can be added to a variety of dishes, enhancing flavor while providing health benefits.

Monitoring and Adjustments

As with all herbal treatments, especially those addressing chronic conditions like heart disease and diabetes, it is vital to monitor the effects closely. Regular consultations with healthcare providers, including blood tests and heart health assessments, will help ensure that the herbal regimen complements other treatments and dietary measures.

Herbs offer a complementary avenue for managing some of the most common chronic conditions affecting people today. By understanding and utilizing the specific properties of these powerful natural medicines, individuals can enhance their heart health and manage diabetes more effectively, leading to improved overall health and quality of life. As always, the integration of these herbs should be done under the guidance of healthcare professionals, ensuring safety and efficacy in their use.

4. Natural Treatments for Respiratory Health

Autoimmune disorders represent a complex and often challenging category of chronic conditions where the body's immune system mistakenly attacks its own tissues. While conventional treatments typically focus on managing symptoms through immunosuppressive medications, an increasing number of individuals are turning to herbal medicine as a supportive and complementary approach. This pivot reflects a broader desire to engage in holistic wellness practices that align more closely with nature and potentially offer fewer side effects.

Understanding autoimmune disorders through the lens of herbalism involves acknowledging the unique complexity of each individual's immune response. Herbs in this context are used not only for their ability to modulate immune system activity but also to address the inflammation, fatigue, and other systemic symptoms that are hallmarks of these conditions.

Adaptogens are a class of herbs renowned for their ability to help the body adapt to stress and bring the body back to a state of homeostasis, which is crucial in managing autoimmune disorders. These herbs are particularly valuable because they can modulate immune function—either enhancing it when necessary or suppressing it when it's overactive. This dual action makes adaptogens an invaluable resource in the herbal toolkit for autoimmune conditions.

- **Ashwagandha (Withania somnifera)**: Often celebrated for its anti-inflammatory and antioxidant properties, ashwagandha helps to reduce the chronic stress that can trigger or exacerbate autoimmune reactions. By supporting adrenal health and modulating the release of stress hormones, it helps to maintain a more balanced immune response.

- **Rhodiola (Rhodiola rosea)**: This herb is not only effective in enhancing physical and mental stamina but also in reducing fatigue, which is a common complaint among those with autoimmune diseases. Rhodiola works by influencing key neurotransmitters involved in mood and energy levels, including serotonin and dopamine, which can be particularly beneficial for those struggling with the emotional stress of managing a chronic condition.

- **Holy Basil (Ocimum sanctum)**: Also known as Tulsi, holy basil functions as an immunomodulator that helps regulate inflammatory processes in the body. Its efficacy in lowering stress is also critical in autoimmune management, as stress reduction can significantly impact immune function.

Chronic inflammation is a symptom often associated with autoimmune disorders. Herbal treatments can provide relief by naturally reducing inflammation levels, thereby alleviating pain and swelling.

- **Turmeric (Curcuma longa)**: With its active compound curcumin, turmeric is highly regarded for its potent anti-inflammatory effects. Regular consumption of turmeric can help reduce the systemic inflammation common in autoimmune disorders, thus easing symptoms and potentially decreasing the need for higher doses of pharmaceutical anti-inflammatories.

- **Ginger (Zingiber officinale)**: Similar to turmeric, ginger possesses significant anti-inflammatory properties. It also serves as an analgesic, making it effective in managing pain and discomfort associated with autoimmune conditions.

- **Boswellia (Boswellia serrata)**: Often used in traditional medicine for its anti-inflammatory and pain-relieving properties, Boswellia is particularly effective in treating conditions like rheumatoid arthritis and inflammatory bowel diseases. Its ability to inhibit pro-inflammatory substances in the body makes it a valuable addition to any herbal regimen for autoimmune management.

The gut plays a critical role in immune system function, and a significant portion of immune activity is located in the gastrointestinal tract. Herbs that support gut health can indirectly influence the progression and symptoms of autoimmune disorders by fostering a healthy gut microbiome and enhancing the integrity of the gut lining.

- **Slippery Elm (Ulmus rubra)**: This herb contains mucilage, a substance that becomes a slick gel when mixed with water. Slippery Elm coats and soothes the mouth, throat, stomach, and intestines, making it incredibly beneficial for gastrointestinal health, which in turn supports immune balance.

- **Marshmallow Root (Althaea officinalis)**: Similar to slippery elm, marshmallow root offers a protective lining to the digestive tract. It helps soothe mucous membranes and supports healthy gut function, which is essential for modulating immune responses in autoimmune conditions.

Chronic fatigue is a significant challenge for individuals with autoimmune diseases. Certain herbs can invigorate the body and enhance energy levels without the side effects often associated with stimulants.

- **Ginseng (Panax ginseng)**: Known for its energizing properties, ginseng can help improve stamina and endurance. It is particularly useful for those whose autoimmune symptoms include chronic fatigue and lethargy.

- **Licorice Root (Glycyrrhiza glabra)**: By supporting adrenal function and maintaining a more consistent level of cortisol in the body, licorice root can help manage fatigue and enhance energy levels. However, due to its potent effects on the body's hormone balance, licorice should be used under the guidance of a knowledgeable practitioner, particularly in those with hypertension.

In integrating herbal therapies into a treatment plan for autoimmune disorders, it is essential to consider each individual's unique medical history, current health status, and any medications they may be taking. Collaborating with healthcare providers, including those trained in both conventional and herbal medicine, ensures a safe and effective approach to managing these complex conditions. While herbs offer a gentle and natural path to symptom relief and immune modulation, they should complement rather than replace conventional treatments prescribed by medical professionals.

When crisis strikes, being prepared with an emergency herbal protocol can be as crucial as a well-stocked first aid kit. In this chapter, we delve into the world of herbal preparations that can be swiftly deployed in times of need—whether for acute injuries, sudden illnesses, or stress reactions. These natural remedies are not just about having the right herbs on hand; they're about knowing how to use them effectively under pressure.

Emergency herbal protocols offer a form of empowerment—a way to take action when professional medical help may not be immediately available. From soothing burns with aloe vera to halting an infection with echinacea, or managing panic with chamomile, these remedies provide effective, time-honored solutions that can be a lifeline in unexpected situations.

In these pages, you will find not only recipes and remedies but also strategies for assembling an emergency herbal response kit that is both comprehensive and compact enough to carry on the go. Equipping yourself with this knowledge and preparation can transform anxiety into confidence, turning herbal wisdom into a potent tool for crisis management.

1. Creating an Emergency Herbal Response Kit

The creation of an Emergency Herbal Response Kit is akin to preparing a lifeboat; it may never need to be used, but its presence provides a profound sense of security. This kit combines the wisdom of traditional herbalism with the practicalities of modern emergency preparedness, ensuring that you're equipped not only with conventional first aid items but also with natural remedies that can provide immediate relief in various crisis situations.

Selecting the Right Container

Choosing the right container for your herbal response kit is the first step. It should be durable, waterproof, and compact enough to be portable but spacious enough to hold all necessary items. A hard-shell case with multiple compartments is ideal as it protects the contents and keeps them organized.

Herbs and Remedies to Include

Your kit should be tailored to cover a broad range of emergencies, including injuries, acute illnesses, and stress reactions. Here's a list of essential herbal remedies to include:

- **Calendula Salve:** Excellent for treating cuts, scrapes, and burns. Calendula has anti-inflammatory properties that promote healing and reduce infection risk.
- **Echinacea Tincture:** Known for its immune-boosting properties, it can be taken at the first sign of infection or when you feel a cold coming on.
- **Peppermint Essential Oil:** Useful for headaches, nausea, and respiratory issues. It can be inhaled to relieve sinus congestion or diluted and applied topically to alleviate headache pain.
- **Activated Charcoal:** For emergency detoxification in cases of ingestion of toxins, activated charcoal can adsorb a wide range of substances.
- **Lavender Essential Oil:** Known for its calming effects, it can be used to relieve stress, anxiety, and insomnia. It also helps in treating burns and stings.
- **Ginger Capsules:** Effective against nausea, motion sickness, and digestion issues. Ginger is a must-have for any emergency kit.
- **Chamomile Tea:** Ideal for calming down during a stressful situation or to help with sleep during unsettling times.
- **Arnica Gel:** For bruises, sprains, and muscle soreness, arnica can help reduce swelling and pain without the side effects of synthetic painkillers.
- **Aloe Vera Gel:** For burns, sunburns, and skin irritations, aloe vera provides cooling relief and aids in skin recovery.

Tools and Supplies

In addition to herbal remedies, your kit should include several essential tools and supplies:

- **Small Scissors and Tweezers:** For cutting bandages or removing splinters.
- **Cotton Balls and Swabs:** For applying salves and tinctures.
- **Bandages and Sterile Gauze:** For covering wounds.
- **Disposable Gloves:** To maintain cleanliness and prevent infection.

While the basics cover a wide range of situations, personalizing your emergency herbal kit based on specific health conditions or known allergies within your family or travel group is crucial. For instance, if someone has a known susceptibility to respiratory issues, including a herbal respiratory syrup or additional peppermint and eucalyptus oils may be wise.

Equally important as the contents of the kit is knowing how to use them effectively. Familiarize yourself with the purposes and applications of each item in your kit. A small booklet with quick usage guidelines for each remedy can be invaluable in an emergency.

To ensure your kit remains effective and ready to use, regular checks are necessary. Replace any products that are past their expiration date and replenish any supplies that have been used. It's a good practice to review the kit's contents every six months.

Consider taking courses in herbal medicine and basic first aid if you haven't already. The more you know about handling medical emergencies and using herbal remedies safely, the more effective your emergency response will be.

2. Natural Antibiotics in Crisis Situations

In crisis situations, where access to conventional medical resources may be limited, the role of natural antibiotics becomes crucial. These plant-based allies offer powerful antimicrobial properties that can help manage infections until more definitive medical treatment is available. This section delves into the world of natural antibiotics, highlighting how they can be used effectively and safely in emergency contexts.

Natural antibiotics differ from their pharmaceutical counterparts in several ways. While they may not always replace the need for synthetic antibiotics, they can provide significant first-line defense against infection, particularly when synthetic options are not accessible.

Key Natural Antibiotics

Several herbs are known for their strong antibacterial and antiviral properties, making them valuable additions to any emergency herbal protocol.

- **Garlic:** Allicin, the primary active compound in garlic, has been shown to have broad-spectrum antimicrobial properties. It is particularly effective against common bacteria such as Staphylococcus and E. coli, making it invaluable in preventing wound infections.

- **Goldenseal:** Containing berberine, a compound effective against bacteria and fungi, goldenseal is often used to treat skin infections and digestive disturbances that involve bacterial overgrowth.
- **Echinacea:** Known primarily for its immune-boosting effects, echinacea also has properties that can help fight flu and other respiratory infections by supporting white blood cell activity.
- **Tea Tree Oil:** Applied topically, tea tree oil is a potent antiseptic, effective against bacteria, viruses, and fungi, making it ideal for treating cuts, burns, and skin infections.
- **Honey:** Especially Manuka honey, which has been used for centuries for wound care, possessing unique antibacterial properties that help in healing and infection prevention.

Integrating these natural antibiotics into emergency care requires understanding their proper forms and applications to maximize their benefits without exacerbating the situation.

Topical Applications

For wounds and skin infections, topical application is often most appropriate. Here's how some of the natural antibiotics can be applied directly:

- **Garlic paste** can be made by crushing fresh cloves and mixing with a small amount of water or oil to form a paste, which can then be applied to the affected area. Note that garlic can cause skin irritation and should be used carefully, potentially diluted for sensitive skin.
- **Tea tree oil** should be diluted with a carrier oil like coconut or almond oil before being applied to cuts or scrapes to prevent irritation.
- **Honey** can be used as is, applied directly to the wound and covered with a clean dressing, changed daily.

When infections are internal, such as sore throats or gastrointestinal issues, oral administration may be necessary:

- **Echinacea tincture** can be taken orally to help boost the immune system and combat upper respiratory infections.
- **Goldenseal capsules** are beneficial for digestive infections but should be used under guidance, as they can interact with other medications and are not recommended for long-term use.

While natural antibiotics are generally safe when used appropriately, there are several considerations to keep in mind to ensure their safe use:

- **Allergic Reactions:** Always test a small amount of any topical remedy on the skin before full application to check for allergic reactions.

- **Pregnancy and Breastfeeding:** Many herbal treatments are not recommended during pregnancy or breastfeeding. Always consult with a healthcare professional.
- **Interaction with Medications:** Some herbs can interact with prescription medications. If you are taking medication, consult with a healthcare professional about potential interactions.

For practical use, it's wise to include various forms of these herbs in your emergency kit:

- **Tinctures and Extracts:** These concentrated forms are ideal for internal use, requiring only small doses.
- **Oils and Salves:** For immediate topical application, ready-made salves or oils can be more convenient and less messy than raw herbs.

In the context of emergency response, natural antibiotics offer a vital resource for managing infections safely and effectively. By understanding the properties of these plants and their proper application, one can greatly enhance the ability to handle medical crises when conventional healthcare may not be immediately available. This knowledge not only empowers individuals but also underscores the importance of maintaining a holistic approach to health and preparedness.

3. Handling Acute Conditions with Herbs

In the realm of herbal medicine, handling acute conditions effectively with herbs is a skill that combines timely intervention with a deep understanding of plant-based healing. Acute conditions, such as sudden digestive upsets, fever, or minor injuries, demand immediate attention and the correct selection of herbs can significantly mitigate discomfort and prevent complications.

Herbal treatment for acute conditions is grounded in the philosophy of supporting the body's natural healing processes rather than merely suppressing symptoms. This approach encourages the body to work through the ailment with the aid of nature's offerings, promoting a more holistic recovery.

Several herbs are particularly suited for treating acute conditions due to their potent medicinal properties. Here's an insight into some key herbs and their primary uses:

- **Peppermint:** Known for its rapid relief of digestive disturbances, peppermint can ease symptoms of indigestion and nausea. Its antispasmodic properties make it ideal for soothing stomach cramps and reducing gas.
- **Ginger:** This root is a powerhouse for treating nausea, vomiting, and dizziness. Its warming effects are also beneficial for chills associated with colds and flu.
- **Chamomile:** Excellent for its calming properties, chamomile can help alleviate anxiety, insomnia, and mild pain. It's particularly useful for treating issues like menstrual cramps or tension headaches.

- **Elderberry:** As an immune booster, elderberry is effective at the onset of cold or flu symptoms. Its antiviral properties help reduce the severity and duration of infections.
- **Yarrow:** This herb is invaluable for its ability to stop bleeding and promote wound healing. It also helps reduce fevers by inducing sweating, assisting the body in natural detoxification during infections.

When addressing acute conditions with herbs, the method of preparation and the timing of administration are critical.

Immediate Responses

- **Teas and Infusions:** For quick relief from symptoms like nausea, indigestion, or cold, herbal teas are effective. Peppermint tea for digestive issues, ginger tea for nausea, and chamomile tea for sleep or anxiety are quick to prepare and easy to administer.
- **Tinctures and Extracts:** These concentrated forms are useful for conditions that require a more potent dose, administered easily and quickly. Elderberry tincture, for example, can be used at the first sign of flu symptoms.

Topical Applications

- **Salves and Poultices:** For skin-related issues or wounds, herbal salves or poultices made from yarrow or calendula can be applied directly to the affected area to promote healing and reduce the risk of infection.
- **Essential Oils:** Oils such as lavender for stress relief or tea tree oil for antiseptic purposes can be used in aromatherapy or diluted and applied topically to treat various acute symptoms.

Correct dosing is crucial in herbal acute care. Using too little may be ineffective, while too much can cause adverse effects. It's essential to follow recommended doses based on the specific herbs and the age, weight, and health condition of the individual.

- **Children and the Elderly:** Special consideration is needed when treating vulnerable populations such as children or the elderly. Lower doses should be used, and certain potent herbs should be avoided.
- **Allergic Reactions and Interactions:** Always consider possible allergic reactions and check for interactions with other medications the individual might be taking.

Understanding how to use herbs effectively during acute conditions is as important as having them on hand. Education on the properties, uses, and contraindications of common emergency herbs should be a priority.

- **Workshops and Courses:** Participating in workshops or courses on herbal medicine can equip individuals with the knowledge needed to handle acute conditions safely.
- **Resource Materials:** Keeping resource materials such as books or quick-reference guides in

the emergency kit can provide crucial information in a pinch.

Handling acute conditions with herbs is an art that enhances the resilience of individuals and communities, providing them with tools to manage unexpected health issues naturally and effectively. This approach not only empowers but also aligns with a holistic view of health, emphasizing prevention and natural care. By cultivating a deeper understanding and respect for herbal remedies, one can tap into the profound healing potential of the natural world.

4. Managing Severe Allergic Reactions with Herbs

In the realm of emergency herbal protocols, managing severe allergic reactions stands out as a critical area where timely, informed action can make a significant difference. Allergic reactions, particularly the severe form known as anaphylaxis, can escalate quickly, posing immediate health threats. While conventional medicine typically relies on antihistamines and epinephrine to counteract these reactions, certain herbs have been recognized for their potential to support and sometimes alleviate allergic symptoms when medical resources are not immediately accessible.

Allergic reactions occur when the body's immune system overreacts to a substance it perceives as harmful, even though it might be innocuous. This can lead to symptoms ranging from mild itching and hives to severe swelling, difficulty breathing, and shock. In an emergency herbal setting, the goal is to moderate the immune system's response and alleviate the symptoms, providing critical time to seek more comprehensive medical treatment.

Several herbs are noted for their natural antihistamine properties, which can help mitigate the body's allergic response by blocking or reducing the production of histamines.

- **Stinging Nettle (Urtica dioica)**: Ironically, nettle, which can induce an allergic reaction when touched, is a potent antihistamine when ingested. Nettle has been used historically to treat hay fever, hives, and other allergic conditions. It can be prepared as a freeze-dried supplement for acute allergic reactions, providing relief from the itching and swelling associated with histamine release.

- **Quercetin**: This natural compound found in many plants and foods boasts excellent anti-inflammatory and antioxidant properties, making it effective against allergic reactions. Quercetin stabilizes mast cells (which release histamine) and can help manage both the symptoms and onset of allergic reactions. It is often taken in supplement form and can be particularly effective when combined with vitamin C, which enhances its anti-allergenic potential.

- **Butterbur (Petasites hybridus)**: Studies have shown that butterbur can be as effective as some over-the-counter antihistamines without the drowsiness. It is especially useful in treating allergic symptoms affecting the respiratory system, such as wheezing and nasal congestion.

The adrenal glands play a crucial role during allergic reactions by producing corticosteroids that help regulate inflammation and immune response. Supporting adrenal health is therefore pivotal in managing allergies.

- **Licorice Root (Glycyrrhiza glabra)**: Licorice acts similarly to corticosteroids, helping to prolong the action of cortisol, the body's natural steroid. This can be beneficial in managing the inflammation associated with allergic reactions. However, licorice should be used judiciously and not on a prolonged basis, as it can affect blood pressure and potassium levels.
- **Turmeric (Curcuma longa)**: Known for its potent curcumin content, turmeric is a powerful anti-inflammatory that can reduce symptoms during allergic reactions, especially those involving respiratory distress.

In cases of anaphylaxis, the respiratory system is often severely affected. Several herbs can aid in keeping airways open and reducing swelling until medical help is available.

- **Ephedra (Ephedra sinica)**: Historically used in traditional Chinese medicine, ephedra has been a go-to herb for treating asthma and bronchial issues. It acts as a bronchodilator, helping to open airways; however, its use must be carefully monitored due to its potent effects and legal status in various regions.
- **Lobelia (Lobelia inflata)**: Often referred to as Indian tobacco, lobelia acts as a strong antispasmodic and bronchodilator, making it useful in treating acute asthma attacks and other respiratory difficulties related to allergic reactions. It should be used under the guidance of a health professional due to its strength and potential toxicity at high doses.

For those prone to severe allergic reactions, having a well-prepared herbal kit can be life-saving. This kit should include herbal antihistamines and anti-inflammatories, quick-access remedies for respiratory distress, and clear instructions on the use of each herb. Additionally, personalizing the kit to include herbs that have proven effective for the individual's specific allergic symptoms can enhance its efficacy. Given the unpredictability and potential severity of allergic reactions, these herbal interventions are intended to complement, not replace, standard medical treatments like epinephrine. They are best used when immediate medical response is delayed or unavailable. Always discuss any herbal regimen with a healthcare provider, especially when dealing with severe allergies, to ensure safety and appropriateness. Incorporating herbs into the management of allergic reactions involves a deep respect for both the power of nature and the complexities of the human body's immune system. By understanding and utilizing these natural remedies, individuals seeking holistic emergency solutions can feel more empowered and prepared to handle severe allergic reactions responsibly.

Embarking on the journey of cultivating medicinal plants is a profound step towards embracing self-sufficiency and deepening one's connection with nature. This chapter opens the gate to a garden where each plant and herb is more than just foliage; they are living pharmacies capable of healing and nurturing the body and mind. Growing your own medicinal plants is not only a practical endeavor that ensures a fresh, reliable supply of herbal remedies but also a transformative experience that enriches one's understanding of natural medicine.

Here, we explore how to establish and maintain a medicinal garden, from the soil up to the harvest. You'll learn how to select plants that suit your health needs and environmental conditions, how to nurture them through organic practices, and ultimately, how to harvest and utilize your homegrown remedies safely and effectively. This guide is tailored to empower both novice gardeners and seasoned green thumbs with the knowledge to create a flourishing herbal sanctuary that supports both the health of the gardener and the planet. Whether you have a small patio or expansive backyard, this chapter transforms it into a therapeutic landscape, fostering a life of health independence and herbal mastery.

1. Advanced Growing Techniques for Medicinal Herbs

In the journey of a prepper herbalist, advancing your growing techniques for medicinal herbs represents a natural evolution of both your garden and your expertise. As you gain more experience, the simple rows of chamomile and pots of lavender that once filled your space evolve into a more complex and productive ecosystem, tailored to both your needs and those of the plants you nurture. This approach not only increases the yield and potency of your herbal remedies but also enhances the sustainability and resilience of your garden.

Embracing Permaculture Principles

Permaculture, a system of agricultural and social design principles centered around simulating or directly utilizing the patterns and features observed in natural ecosystems, offers profound insights into how we can cultivate medicinal herbs more effectively. Unlike traditional gardening, which often involves planting in isolated plots, permaculture integrates the land, resources, people, and the environment into synergistic systems that produce food and medicine sustainably. One of the core concepts of permaculture is the design of **polycultures**, where multiple plants are grown together to mutually benefit one another. In a medicinal herb garden, this might mean planting garlic among your roses to deter pests naturally, or growing chamomile alongside your vegetables to attract beneficial insects and improve soil health. This diversity not only reduces disease but also enhances the overall productivity and ecological balance of your garden.

Soil Health and Its Importance

The foundation of any successful garden is its soil. Advanced growing techniques focus heavily on improving and maintaining robust soil health. Healthy soil contains a living, breathing community of organisms, each playing a role in decomposing organic material and making nutrients available to plants. This ecosystem needs to be fed and cared for, much like the plants themselves.

To enrich your soil, integrate organic matter regularly. This could be in the form of compost, aged manure, or green mulches. Additionally, practices like **crop rotation** and **cover cropping** can significantly enhance soil fertility. Cover crops such as clover or alfalfa can fix nitrogen in the soil, reducing the need for chemical fertilizers and improving soil structure.

Advanced Water Management Techniques

Efficient water use is crucial in sustainable gardening. Techniques like **drip irrigation** and **rainwater harvesting** not only conserve water but ensure that plants get moisture directly to their roots, where it's most needed. Mulching plays a pivotal role here, helping retain moisture in the soil, reducing evaporation, and also suppressing weed growth that would otherwise compete with your herbs for water.

The Role of Microclimates

Every garden is full of microclimates, small areas where the conditions differ slightly from the surrounding area. Recognizing and utilizing these microclimates can significantly enhance your growing potential. For instance, a wall that retains heat well could be a perfect spot for heat-loving herbs like basil and thyme, while a shaded area might better support moisture-loving plants like mint.

Propagation Techniques for Sustainability

Propagation—growing new plants from seeds, cuttings, or divisions—is a fundamental skill for any gardener wishing to deepen their practice. By mastering these techniques, you can ensure a continuous supply of medicinal herbs:

- **Seed Saving:** Harvesting and storing seeds from your best plants not only saves money but also helps develop plant strains that are well-adapted to your local conditions.
- **Cuttings:** Many herbs, such as rosemary and lavender, can be easily propagated from cuttings. This method allows you to quickly expand your garden and share plants with others in your community.
- **Division:** Perennial herbs like chives and horseradish can be propagated by dividing their roots or bulbs. This not only helps to control the size of the plants but also invigorates them and increases their lifespan.

In today's world, technology can also play a part in enhancing our gardening techniques. Soil moisture sensors, automatic watering systems, and solar-powered growing lights can all make managing a medicinal herb garden more efficient, especially for those balancing gardening with other responsibilities.

As herbalists, our connection to the land is deeply rooted in respect and stewardship. Ethical cultivation practices such as **sustainable harvesting**, **seed sharing**, and **biodiversity preservation** are not just beneficial in practical terms but are crucial in maintaining the integrity and sustainability of our herbal practices. These practices ensure that as we benefit from the earth, we also contribute to its health, preserving a balance that supports both our gardens and the wider ecosystem.

By adopting these advanced growing techniques, your medicinal herb garden will not only flourish but also become a dynamic and sustainable component of your self-reliant lifestyle. Each plant that thrives under your care brings with it a deeper understanding of both the natural world and the incredible potential of herbs as partners in our health and well-being.

2. Creating a Year-Round Herbal Supply

Creating a year-round herbal supply is an empowering step for any prepper herbalist. It ensures that you have access to essential medicinal herbs regardless of the season, fostering a deeper level of self-reliance and readiness. This endeavor requires thoughtful planning, an understanding of the life cycles of various herbs, and innovative approaches to growing and storing your herbal bounty.

To maintain a constant supply of medicinal herbs, it's crucial to understand the life cycles of the plants you're cultivating. Annuals, biennials, and perennials each have their own growth patterns and needs:

- **Annuals** such as basil and cilantro complete their life cycle in one year and must be replanted annually. They often yield a quick harvest and can be grown in succession to provide continuous output.

- **Biennials** like parsley and angelica take two years to complete their life cycle, typically forming leaves in the first year and flowering in the second. Planning for biennials involves allowing them to seed and regenerate.

- **Perennials**, such as mint and oregano, return year after year from the same roots. Once established, they require less planting but might need division and rejuvenation to keep them vigorous.

To achieve a year-round supply, integrate a mix of these plant types and tailor your planting schedule to your specific climate zone. Here are some strategies to consider:

- **Start Early Indoors:** For a head start on the growing season, begin sowing seeds indoors under grow lights or on a sunny windowsill. This is especially useful for slower-growing or tender herbs that need more time to mature before transplanting outdoors.

- **Succession Planting:** Plant new seeds or seedlings at intervals throughout the growing season to ensure a continuous harvest. This method works exceptionally well with fast-growing herbs like dill and cilantro.

- **Extend the Season:** Use cold frames, greenhouses, or hoop houses to protect herbs from early frost or to extend the growing season into the cooler months. This can be particularly effective for perennial herbs that benefit from a longer growing period.

Creating optimal conditions for each herb is key to their health and productivity. Most herbs thrive in full sun with well-draining soil, but some, like lemon balm and mint, prefer a bit of shade. Enhance soil quality by adding compost and organic matter, ensuring that nutrients are available to support plant growth year-round.

Not all herbs need to be grown in the ground. Many adapt well to container gardening, which can be an excellent option for managing herbs that require different soil conditions or for those living in urban settings without traditional garden space.

- **Indoor Gardening:** Some herbs can be grown indoors year-round, provided they have enough light. Consider setting up a designated herb area near a south-facing window or invest in a quality grow light to provide sufficient lumens.

- **Hydroponics and Aquaponics:** These soil-less growing systems can be set up indoors to produce a substantial amount of herbs. They are particularly useful for culinary herbs like basil and parsley, which require consistent moisture and nutrient levels, both of which are meticulously controlled in these systems.

To ensure that your herbal supply extends beyond the growing season, proper harvesting and storage techniques are crucial:

- **Harvest Timing:** Collect herbs at their peak potency, which is usually just before they flower when their essential oils are most concentrated. Dry them quickly to preserve their medicinal qualities.

- **Drying Herbs:** Use a dehydrator, air dry in a warm, dry place, or even an oven on a low setting to dry herbs efficiently. Store dried herbs in airtight containers away from light and heat to maintain their potency.

- **Freezing Herbs:** Many herbs can be frozen, retaining much of their flavor and therapeutic properties. Freeze them in water using ice cube trays or process them into pestos and sauces that can be defrosted and used as needed.

- **Making Tinctures and Oils:** Transform herbs into tinctures, oils, or salves, which not only preserve the herbs but also make them easy to use medicinally throughout the year.

Finally, part of sustaining a year-round herbal supply involves community engagement. Sharing seeds, cuttings, and knowledge with fellow gardeners can help diversify your herbal collection and increase resilience. Participate in seed swaps and plant sharing programs to expand your garden's diversity and robustness.

By implementing these strategies, you build not just a garden, but a well-rounded, sustainable apothecary that can support you and your community year-round. This approach not only ensures a steady supply of medicinal herbs but also connects you deeply with the cycles of nature and the rhythm of the seasons.

3. Wildcrafting: Ethical Foraging Practices

In the tapestry of skills that a modern herbalist weaves, wildcrafting—the practice of gathering plant materials from their natural, wild habitat—stands out as a deeply rewarding and inherently respectful art. Ethical foraging isn't merely about collecting what you need from the wild; it's about understanding the ecosystem, contributing to its health, and ensuring its continuity for generations to come.

Ethical wildcrafting is rooted in a philosophy that respects nature and recognizes the interconnectedness of life. As herbalists, we step into the wild not as conquerors but as humble students and stewards. Our goal is to harvest in such a way that supports the natural cycles and contributes to the habitat's ongoing vitality.

Before you begin harvesting any plant from the wild, it is crucial to understand the ecosystem in which it thrives. Each plant plays a role in its environment, perhaps providing food for pollinators, offering shelter for small animals, or contributing to the soil's nutrient cycle. A responsible wildcrafter will take the time to study not only the individual species but also their relationships within the ecosystem.

- **Research Local Flora:** Knowing which plants are native, which are invasive, and which are endangered is a fundamental part of ethical foraging. This knowledge ensures that one's foraging practices do not disrupt local biodiversity.

- **Assess Plant Populations:** Only forage plants that are abundant and healthy. If a particular species is not thriving, even if it's not endangered, it's best to leave it alone. This assessment should be ongoing, as plant populations can fluctuate from year to year.

The timing of your harvest can significantly impact the health of the plant population. Harvesting should align with the plant's life cycle to ensure that the plants can continue to propagate and sustain their population.

- **Seasonal Awareness:** Most plants should be harvested when they are most robust, typically just before they are set to flower. This timing ensures that the plants are at their peak in terms of the medicinal qualities we seek, while still allowing them to complete their reproductive cycle.

- **Harvesting Techniques:** Use tools that allow for clean cuts and minimal damage to the plant and its surroundings. For example, when harvesting roots, carefully replace the soil and disturb the area as little as possible. For leaves, flowers, or seeds, ensure that enough remains for the plant to continue its growth and reproduction.

The principle of "leave no trace" is paramount in wildcrafting. This philosophy extends beyond not leaving litter in the natural environment—it's about making sure your presence and activity do not leave any lasting scars on the landscape.

- **Path Management:** Stick to established trails as much as possible to avoid trampling undergrowth and compacting soil.
- **Damage Avoidance:** Be mindful of the surrounding plants and soil structure. Avoid damaging other plants and their root systems when digging for roots and bulbs.

Wildcrafting must always be conducted in accordance with local laws and regulations. Many areas have specific rules about what can be foraged, how much, and at what times of the year. These regulations are often in place to protect local ecosystems and species from overharvesting.

- **Permit Requirements:** Some regions require permits for foraging. Always check and comply with local regulations before you begin harvesting.
- **Indigenous Land Rights:** Recognize and respect the rights of indigenous communities whose land you may wish to forage on. Many plants we use in herbalism are also sacred plants for local indigenous people, and their traditions, needs, and rights should be honored.

Part of being an ethical forager is spreading the word about sustainable practices. Teaching others not only spreads knowledge but also fosters a community of responsible herbalists.

- **Workshops and Walks:** Consider leading educational forays into nature, focusing on plant identification, ecosystem health, and ethical harvesting practices.
- **Mentorship:** If you have the opportunity, mentor less experienced foragers. Sharing your knowledge one-on-one is a powerful way to promote sustainability.

Wildcrafting with respect and thoughtfulness reinforces a symbiotic relationship with nature, where we take only what we need and give back in equal measure. It is an exchange marked not by transaction, but by gratitude and a deep sense of responsibility to the plants that heal us and the earth that hosts us. As we walk through the wilderness with our baskets and shears, let us always be guided by the profound understanding that we are part of a much larger community of life.

4. Leveraging Local Ecosystems for Plant Diversity

Leveraging local ecosystems for plant diversity is not just about planting a garden; it's about creating a vibrant, sustainable habitat that resonates with the natural flora of the area, enhancing both the health of the environment and the potency of its medicinal plants. This practice encourages herbalists and gardeners to think beyond the confines of traditional gardening, promoting a deeper connection with the local landscape and its inherent botanical resources.

When you start to see your garden as part of a larger ecological framework, you begin to appreciate the importance of diversity in plant species. This diversity isn't just beneficial for the garden's ecosystem; it also provides a richer, more resilient source of medicinal plants. Each region has its own set of native plants that have adapted over centuries to thrive in the specific conditions of that area, from soil type and pH to climate and rainfall patterns. By understanding and harnessing these conditions, you can grow a robust medicinal garden that is naturally equipped to thrive and resist pests and diseases.

The first step in this process is to thoroughly understand your local ecosystem. This means learning about the native plants in your area, including their medicinal uses and their roles within the local environment. It also involves understanding the soil types, climate conditions, and the natural fauna that interact with these plants. Many local extension offices and botanical gardens offer resources and classes that can provide valuable insights into the specifics of regional flora.

When selecting plants for your garden, consider those that are native to your area or have similar growing requirements to your local conditions. These plants will naturally be more resistant to local pests and diseases and will require less water and fewer soil amendments to thrive. For example, if you live in a region with a high rainfall, consider plants that are adapted to wet conditions, such as marshmallow (Althaea officinalis) or horsetail (Equisetum arvense).

Additionally, consider the ecological benefits of each plant. Some plants, like echinacea or lavender, attract pollinators, which are vital for maintaining the health of your garden and the larger ecosystem. Others might help improve soil quality or deter pests naturally, reducing the need for chemical interventions.

Incorporating sustainable harvesting practices is crucial when leveraging local ecosystems. This means understanding the growth cycles of the plants you are using and ensuring that you harvest in a way that does not deplete natural populations or harm the environment. For example, never harvest more than a third of a particular plant population, and make sure to leave plenty of seeds or roots for future growth.

If you are foraging wild plants, be especially careful to adhere to ethical guidelines. Only forage plants that are abundant, and avoid those that are rare or endangered. Always have permission to forage if you are on private land or in protected areas.

Building a relationship with the plants you cultivate or forage goes beyond mere gardening or harvesting. Spend time in your garden and in local wild spaces to observe the interactions within plant communities and between plants and other organisms. This connection fosters a greater understanding of the ecological balances in your area and informs your practices both as a gardener and as a herbalist.

Finally, consider how your gardening practices affect the broader ecosystem. Use organic methods whenever possible to avoid introducing harmful chemicals into the environment. Composting plant waste and using it as fertilizer not only reduces waste but also improves soil health, creating a sustainable loop that enhances the overall health of your garden.

Encouraging native wildlife, such as birds, bees, and beneficial insects, by providing natural habitats and food sources can also help maintain the ecological balance, aiding in pollination and the natural control of pests.

In essence, leveraging local ecosystems for plant diversity is about embracing a holistic approach to gardening and herbalism. It involves a commitment to understanding and respecting the natural processes that have shaped the local landscape and flora. By fostering a diverse and ecologically sound garden, you not only enrich your own medicinal resources but also contribute to the health and sustainability of the environment. This approach not only yields a garden that is vibrant and teeming with life but also one that is a dynamic part of the local ecosystem, resilient and rich in the medicinal plants that thrive naturally in its conditions.

In the journey of embracing natural wellness, the collective wisdom and shared experiences of a community can transform individual practices into a powerful movement. Chapter 5 delves into the heart of the prepper's herbal community, exploring how building networks of like-minded individuals can significantly enrich our understanding and application of herbal medicine. As preppers and herbalists, we often focus on personal resilience and self-sufficiency, but it's through our connections with others that our knowledge deepens and our impact broadens.

This chapter celebrates the vibrant tapestry of relationships that form when herbal enthusiasts gather, whether in workshops, community gardens, or online forums. Here, we explore how to cultivate these connections, creating a supportive network that thrives on mutual learning and shared goals. From organizing local meet-ups to exchange seeds and cuttings to collaborating on community herbal gardens that provide medicinal resources for all, this chapter provides a roadmap for nurturing an herbal community that can stand the test of time and crisis.

By fostering these ties, we not only ensure the survival of invaluable herbal knowledge but also reinforce the foundations of a society that values health, sustainability, and the well-being of its members. The prepper's herbal community is not just about preparing for the future—it's about enriching our lives today, together.

1. Building a Network of Herbalists

In the realm of natural medicine, the strength of an individual's knowledge is amplified manifold through the collective wisdom of a community. Building a network of herbalists not only enriches each member's understanding and capabilities but also fosters a resilient support system that can thrive in times of both peace and challenge.

Herbalists, by nature, are connectors — not just of people, but of people to plants, and plants to traditions. However, forming a network goes beyond simple connections; it's about creating meaningful, enduring relationships that encourage exchange, education, and support. These networks can take many forms, from informal groups to structured organizations, each serving different purposes but all crucial to the advancement and preservation of herbal knowledge.

Starting Local: Grassroots Networking

The foundation of any robust herbal network often begins at the local level. Starting small allows members to meet regularly, share resources, and provide immediate support. Here are some practical steps to initiate and grow a local network:

- **Host Meetups:** Regular meetups can be as simple as gathering in a member's home or a community center to discuss herbal topics, exchange seeds, or plan community projects.
- **Workshops and Classes:** Organize workshops that cater to different levels of expertise, from beginner to advanced. These can cover a range of topics such as herbal medicine basics, advanced extraction methods, or specific studies on local plant species.
- **Community Gardens:** Establish a community garden dedicated to medicinal plants. This not only provides a tangible focal point for the community's activities but also serves as a living classroom and resource bank.
- **Herbal Walks:** Arrange guided walks in local natural spaces. These walks, led by knowledgeable herbalists, can help members learn plant identification, ethical wildcrafting practices, and ecological awareness firsthand.

In today's digital age, the scope for building networks extends far beyond local boundaries. Online platforms can bridge herbalists from across the globe, creating a rich tapestry of cultural knowledge and experience.

- **Social Media Groups:** Platforms like Facebook, Instagram, and LinkedIn offer spaces to create interest-based groups where members can share articles, discuss various topics, and coordinate events.
- **Online Forums and Message Boards:** More structured than social media, these platforms can host a wealth of archived knowledge and active discussions that are easily searchable and categorized.

- **Webinars and Online Courses:** These tools not only help in spreading knowledge but also in building a network by connecting herbalists who may be interested in specialized topics not readily available in their local area.

Herbal medicine conferences, symposia, and workshops are excellent venues for networking with a broader community. These events often attract a diverse group of practitioners, educators, and enthusiasts from various parts of the world.

- **Attending Events:** Participation in these events opens up numerous opportunities to meet leaders in the field, learn about the latest research, and discover new techniques and applications.

- **Presenting Papers and Research:** For those who are more deeply involved in the study of herbal medicine, presenting your work at conferences can help establish your reputation in the community and open doors to collaborative opportunities.

- **Vendor Booths:** For herbalists who produce their own products, purchasing a booth at an event can be a great way to get your brand out there and connect with other like-minded businesses and practitioners.

Within any network, the flow of knowledge is pivotal. Experienced herbalists mentoring newcomers creates a nurturing environment that ensures the transmission of not just knowledge but also values and ethical practices.

- **Formal Apprenticeships:** These are structured programs where novices work closely with experienced herbalists, gaining hands-on experience and in-depth knowledge.

- **Informal Mentorship:** This can be as simple as more experienced members providing guidance and support to newer herbalists within the community.

Collaborative projects, whether they are research studies, community health initiatives, or conservation efforts, can solidify networks by working towards common goals. These projects harness the diverse skills of their members and often achieve results that are far greater than the sum of their parts.

Finally, one of the most profound ways a network of herbalists can impact their broader community is through education. Offering free or low-cost classes to the public on the basics of herbal medicine not only demystifies the subject but also empowers more people to take charge of their health, promoting wellness and resilience within the community.

Building a network of herbalists is about crafting a web of relationships that are rooted in respect, driven by passion, and dedicated to the growth and sustainability of herbal practices. It's these connections that will carry the rich traditions of herbal medicine forward, making them accessible and relevant for future generations.

2. Teaching Herbal Medicine Skills

In any community, the ability to teach and pass on knowledge not only enriches the group but also fortifies it against future uncertainties. Teaching herbal medicine within the prepper's herbal community goes beyond the transmission of traditional knowledge—it transforms ordinary members into empowered healers and educators, capable of sustaining their own health and that of those around them. Here, we explore how to effectively teach herbal medicine skills, ensuring that this vital knowledge flourishes in any community setting.

A teacher in the context of herbal medicine is not just an instructor but a guide and a mentor. The responsibility involves not only the transmission of factual knowledge but also the cultivation of intuition, observation, and ethical practices among students. A great teacher inspires curiosity and confidence, allowing students to explore and learn in ways that resonate most deeply with them.

Designing a curriculum for teaching herbal medicine should start with a clear understanding of the goals and needs of your community. Are you addressing beginners or those with some experience? Are the classes for general interest or aimed at developing professional level skills? Here's how you can structure an effective curriculum:

- **Basics First:** Begin with the fundamentals of herbal medicine, including identification of plants, understanding their medicinal properties, and learning how to harvest them responsibly.

- **Practical Skills:** Introduce practical skills such as making tinctures, salves, and teas. This hands-on experience is crucial for embedding knowledge and building confidence.

- **Advanced Studies:** For more advanced students, delve into complex topics such as the biochemistry of herbs, advanced extraction methods, and the treatment of specific ailments.

- **Continuous Assessment:** Provide opportunities for feedback and assessment, helping students gauge their progress and encouraging them to explore areas for further study.

The effectiveness of teaching herbal medicine greatly depends on the methods employed. Different settings and tools can be utilized to cater to diverse learning styles:

- **Workshops and Seminars:** These are ideal for delivering hands-on experience and for engaging directly with students, allowing for immediate feedback and adjustment.

- **Field Trips:** Organize trips to natural habitats or botanical gardens. Such excursions allow students to see plants in their natural settings, which is invaluable for their botanical identification skills and understanding of ecological relationships.

- **Online Platforms:** Use online courses and webinars to reach a wider audience. This method is particularly useful for theoretical topics and can be a convenient way for students to learn at their own pace.

- **Community Teaching Gardens:** Establish a garden specifically for educational purposes. It can serve as a living classroom for students to practice cultivation, harvesting, and direct application of their herbal knowledge.

Engaging the Community

Teaching shouldn't be limited to formal settings. Engaging with the broader community through public lectures, free clinics, and participation in local health fairs can raise awareness and interest in herbal medicine. Such activities not only teach herbal skills but also build a supportive network that values and understands the importance of this knowledge.

Mentorship Programs

Mentorship is a cornerstone of traditional herbal medicine education. Pairing less experienced members with seasoned herbalists allows for personalized guidance and deeper learning. This relationship can be particularly empowering, providing newcomers with the confidence to experiment and refine their skills under supervision.

Documentation and Resources

Encourage the documentation of lessons learned, recipes tried, and remedies created. Keeping a community archive or library not only preserves knowledge but also allows it to be continuously updated and refined by future generations. This resource can become a vital tool in the community's ongoing education and resilience.

Ethical Considerations

Teaching herbal medicine also involves instilling a strong ethical foundation. Discuss the implications of wildcrafting, the importance of sustainability, and the responsibilities of an herbalist to their community. It's essential that students understand the broader impact of their practice, both ecologically and socially.

Evaluating Impact

Finally, regularly evaluate the impact of your teaching efforts. Are students able to effectively use the skills they've learned? How has the community's health and well-being been enhanced by these efforts? Feedback from students and community members can provide valuable insights that help refine teaching methods and curriculum.

Teaching herbal medicine within a prepper's community is an enriching endeavor that strengthens communal ties and ensures a legacy of health and resilience. Through thoughtful, well-structured education programs, every community member can become a link in a chain of knowledge that not only survives but thrives through generations.

3. Preserving Herbal Knowledge for Future Generations

In the vast journey of herbalism, one of the most vital endeavors is the preservation of herbal knowledge for future generations. As practitioners and stewards of this ancient craft, it is our duty and privilege to ensure that the wisdom we gather about medicinal plants and their uses is not lost but rather enhanced and handed down through the ages. This chapter focuses on methods to safeguard and perpetuate this invaluable resource, ensuring that our descendants have the tools they need to lead healthier, more sustainable lives.

The first step in preserving herbal knowledge is meticulous documentation. In our digital age, there are more ways than ever to record and store information securely and accessibly:

- **Digital Archives:** Creating digital documents that can be easily updated and shared is crucial. These archives should include detailed descriptions of plant properties, cultivation methods, harvesting times, medicinal uses, and recipes for remedies.

- **Blogs and Online Journals:** Regularly contributing to a blog or online journal can serve as a dynamic platform for sharing knowledge. These entries not only document herbal wisdom but also invite community interaction, feedback, and contribution.

- **Video Tutorials:** In an era where visual learning is predominant, creating video tutorials on herbal identification, preparation techniques, and usage tips can capture the practical aspects of herbalism in a way that written descriptions cannot.

Education is the cornerstone of knowledge preservation. By setting up structured educational programs, we can ensure a continuous, systematic transfer of knowledge:

- **Herbal Schools:** Establishing or affiliating with schools dedicated to the study of herbal medicine provides a formal avenue for education, from introductory courses to advanced clinical training.

- **Workshops and Retreats:** Short-term educational experiences such as workshops or retreats can offer intensive, hands-on learning opportunities about specific aspects of herbal medicine. These are especially valuable for community members who may not be able to commit to long-term study.

- **Youth Programs:** Integrating herbal knowledge into programs for children and teenagers ensures early exposure to herbal practices. This not only aids in early learning but also helps ingrain a respect for nature and natural medicine from a young age.

Engaging the community is essential for the longevity of herbal knowledge. Community involvement ensures that herbalism isn't kept in the hands of a few but is shared widely among many, increasing the knowledge base and diversity of applications.

- **Community Gardens:** These gardens serve as both a practical and educational resource, allowing community members to learn about growing, harvesting, and using medicinal plants.

- **Health Fairs and Symposia:** Participating in local health fairs or symposia as speakers or exhibitors can help raise awareness about the benefits of herbal medicine and educate the public on how to use herbs safely and effectively.
- **Volunteer Programs:** Encouraging experienced herbalists to volunteer in schools, community centers, and senior centers can spread knowledge and practical skills throughout the community.

Incorporating herbal knowledge into the cultural fabric of the community helps ensure its preservation. This can be achieved by celebrating herbal traditions through festivals, books, and storytelling, making herbalism a living part of community identity.

- **Herbal Festivals:** Organize or participate in festivals that celebrate herbal traditions, featuring workshops, stalls, and discussions about medicinal plants. These events can help to ignite interest and pride in local herbal heritage.
- **Publication of Books and Guides:** Writing and publishing comprehensive guides on local flora and their medicinal uses can serve as permanent records of herbal knowledge. Encourage local herbalists to contribute to these publications to ensure a broad spectrum of knowledge and experience is covered.
- **Storytelling:** Engage elders and long-time herbalists to share their stories and experiences with younger generations through oral storytelling, an age-old method of knowledge transmission that can convey nuances and insights not captured in written form.

As we strive to preserve herbal knowledge, it is equally important to consider the legal and ethical aspects:

- **Intellectual Property Rights:** Navigate the complexities of intellectual property laws when documenting and sharing herbal knowledge to ensure that original sources are credited and that the information is used ethically.
- **Conservation Efforts:** Work with local and national conservation groups to ensure that the plants we depend on are protected from overharvesting and habitat destruction. This includes advocating for sustainable wildcrafting and cultivation practices.

Preserving herbal knowledge for future generations is a multi-faceted endeavor that requires commitment, creativity, and cooperation. By documenting and sharing our wisdom, educating young and old, involving the community, integrating herbal practices into our culture, and navigating ethical considerations, we ensure that this ancient art not only survives but thrives.

4. Promoting Community Health Initiatives through Herbalism

Promoting community health initiatives through herbalism is a profound way to integrate traditional knowledge with modern health needs, creating a resilient, informed, and health-empowered community. In areas where healthcare may be limited or during times of crisis, herbal medicine offers sustainable support, alleviating the strain on medical facilities and providing basic healthcare to the populace. This integration requires a systematic approach that includes education, collaboration with health professionals, and the establishment of community-supported herbal gardens and health programs.

The cornerstone of promoting herbalism in community health initiatives is education. By offering workshops, courses, and seminars on herbal medicine, communities can awaken a widespread interest and understanding of the role that herbs can play in maintaining health. These educational programs should cover a variety of topics, including the basics of identifying, harvesting, and using medicinal plants, understanding their benefits and limitations, and recognizing when professional medical treatment is necessary.

Educational efforts should also focus on training individuals who can then teach others, creating a multiplying effect that can reach a broader audience. These community leaders or herbal educators need not only a deep understanding of herbal medicine but also the ability to communicate this knowledge effectively, ensuring that it is accessible and applicable to people of all ages and backgrounds.

For herbalism to gain a foothold in community health initiatives, establishing a strong relationship with healthcare professionals is essential. This collaboration bridges the gap between traditional and conventional medicine, providing a more integrated approach to health that can be especially powerful in underserved areas.

Herbal practitioners and healthcare providers can work together to create guidelines that safely incorporate herbal remedies with conventional treatments, offering a comprehensive resource for community health workers. Such collaborations can also lead to community health drives and screenings where herbal preventive measures and treatments are introduced under professional supervision, ensuring safety and efficacy.

Establishing community herbal gardens is a practical approach to promoting herbalism. These gardens serve as both educational and resource hubs, where community members can learn about the growth, care, and use of medicinal plants. Community gardens can also be therapeutic spaces for individuals to connect with nature and each other, fostering a sense of community and shared purpose. Furthermore, these gardens can act as a source of local, sustainable medicine that can be used to support public health, particularly in times of economic difficulty or medical supply shortages. They can also encourage discussions about nutrition and holistic health practices, extending the health benefits beyond herbal medicine.

For herbalism to be recognized as a viable part of community health initiatives, it needs to be integrated into local health policies. Advocates for herbal medicine should engage with policy makers to draft proposals that recognize and regulate the use of herbal medicines. This could include funding for herbal medicine research, inclusion of herbal treatments in community health centers, and the development of regulations that ensure the quality and safety of herbs available to the public.

To ensure the sustainability of herbal health initiatives, ongoing outreach efforts are necessary. These should aim to keep the community engaged and informed about the benefits and developments in herbal medicine. Regular updates through local media, newsletters, and social media can keep the conversation going and the community involved.

Creating special interest groups or clubs can also maintain interest and participation in herbal practices. These groups can spearhead efforts to explore new herbs, start new garden projects, or expand educational outreach, ensuring that herbalism remains a dynamic and integral part of community health.

Promoting community health initiatives through herbalism not only involves educating the public and collaborating with health professionals but also integrating these practices into the fabric of community life. By establishing herbal gardens, engaging in policy advocacy, and ensuring continual outreach and education, communities can enhance their resilience, self-sufficiency, and overall health. These efforts lay the groundwork for a sustainable health model that honors traditional knowledge while addressing modern health challenges, making herbalism a cornerstone of community health strategy.

SCAN QR CODE TO DOWNLOAD YOUR BONUS

Made in the USA
Columbia, SC
18 December 2024